I0099406

VISUAL ENCOUNTERS

By

Ellen Marie Blend

Visual Encounters

A LeasCon Book

Copyright ©️ 1999 by Ellen Marie Blend

All rights reserved by U.S. Government Copyright laws.
Published in the United States by Image Ink Publications.

Illustrations by Lawri J. Mitchell
Copyright ©️ 1999 *Lawri* /Mitchell West Design

Copy edited by Pamela M. Green

Library of Congress Number: 99-95276

ISBN: 1-929219-00-8
     978-1-929219001

First printing: October 1999
Second printing: March 2009
Third printing: July 2017

Public Notification:
All names have been changed to protect the privacy of
those cited and to avoid any ensuing controversies.

Acknowledgment

I would particularly like to acknowledge my deceased friend, Gwenn, of many years. She was fully responsible for helping me grow in the area of spiritual realms, encouraging me, and never doubting any psychic whim that ever crossed my being. Without her, I could never have written this or any other material. She was my sole interpreter of the visual imagery I conceived. It was with her intuitive connectivity that this writing and other works came to be. For that and much, much more, I thank her.

Psychic Phenomena Books by Ellen Marie Blend

Unraveling the Weave
Looking Back
Conversing on a Higher Level
Impunity from Lunacy – Book One
Impunity from Lunacy – Book Two

Watch for These Titles Coming Soon

Real Objectivity
When is it My Turn?
Spiritually Speaking

Other Books by Ellen Marie Blend

Not About Money
The Educator

PREFACE

This writing is only for those who believe in the higher, little known powers of mental images, or have experienced them in some way as to not think the writer disconnected from reality. For I am reality, and for many years have discarded the passing visual thoughts, silly identifications with colors, and recently numbers, but more specifically "visions" of my mind's eye.

At this writing I am a novice. I am just learning to accept that what I see in my mind's eye has validity. For the most part, the visions are a representation of something, usually symbolic, and I am to understand their meaning either by interpretation or simply by definition.

The problem I have is that I do not interpret well. I have no depth perception; only surface vision. What I see is what I get. I recently read a book about psychic powers, spiritual guides and visions. What it said about visions was that "interpretation" was the most important part! I laughed. "I don't do interpretations. I do visions!"

I was able to laugh because I have a counterpart. She is a friend who is more "reality" than I, an extremely "black and white" sort of person. Over the years that I have known her I have learned to believe in her experiential powers because she is so solidly and seemingly boorish "black and white." On matters of the supernatural powers, however, she is well read, learned, and gleaning of information. She is able to soothe and encourage my questioning mind, give me valid references and explanations to back up my experiences, and most importantly, interpret what I see with utmost accuracy.

The purpose of the dialogue contained in this book is to record what I have learned to date, to let you experience the revelations as I have, and to live with the mystery and mystique as I unravel the truths before us both. We will learn together. What I state to you is what I know at the time of discovery, and as I learn more, so shall you. You will be introduced one by one to my family and friends, and their associated spirits. You will also learn what I have learned about telepathic messages and other transmissions, as I have some to report now in their embryonic stages.

CONTENTS

To my dearest of friends, whom I see in the clearest light, and with the kindest of heart. I speak of you with love.

CHAPTER ONE

Blend of Talent

Two friends, for maybe 15 years now, similar in core foundation and value systems, but having two very distinct personalities, life styles, and talents of higher power. They unite, not in thought, but in information exchange, understanding and respect. Both are attuned to the others' needs, and are there for one another. True friends.

Gwenn is very perceptive. She just "knows," and I've learned to trust her judgment. It is almost impeccable. Extreme tiredness or stress may get her off track, but only then. She is seldom open to receiving information from anyone. "She has made up her mind" to most points of discussion and is rarely willing to hear new information. She is locked into her firm and set beliefs. A small flaw, considering her vast knowledge and ability. She can read and interpret people, situations, surroundings, circumstances and the unknown.

She occasionally seeks an opinion from me or input--and only if I agree with her is it valid; but then, all she is looking for is an "ear" and "approval." As her friend, I listen and give comment; but it is generally rejected because I am off base to her train of thought. She settles her own verbal dispute. Sometimes I get a little angry, feeling, "Can't I ever be right? Or can't you even let me think I'm a little right?," but I let it go, because the important thing is that Gwenn is satisfied with her own answers. Occasionally, I just happen to say the right thing, but that is rare.

In terms of my interpretation, there is almost nothing that she agrees with. For instance, she will present a situation, and I will say something about how or why I think it is that way. Her immediate interjection is "No, . . ." always "No" and then I hear her version. Very seldom do I get "I thought so too," or "That's true," which is what I hear if I ever do get it right. She has already formulated her opinion about the matter, and no other input will be accepted. But, she's usually right; in fact, almost always right.

Together we have learned the differences in our abilities and how we each react to situations. She is extremely "audio." Everything she hears is learned and stored, permanently. She accepts input by listening rather than reading, hearing rather than seeing. Naturally, her skills are based around those attributes.

I am an extremely visual person. I must see it or read it to receive input and understanding. My entire value system is based on what is visually appealing to me, or visually acceptable, and I learn best when I read or write. I must actually see the words.

With these two distinct learning and living lifestyles, together we have discovered a unique blend of talent which has become the foundation of this book. For I am the visionary and she the interpreter. I cannot get accurate readings of what I see without her, and she has no ability to read what she cannot see. My visions have color and sometimes movement, and occasional sounds, but she cannot visualize until I paint the picture verbally. And when I do, a psychic interpretation or reading is then forthcoming, like a miracle. She has a way of questioning me to find the answers needed to solve my mysteries, and when this is accomplished, I know that together we have found a way to communicate on a level one step above the norm.

CHAPTER TWO

Breakdown

Returning to work after both of my children were born was not just a good idea, it was essential. The extra money was nice, but not nearly as important as my mental health. I had become so depressed. In hindsight I learned that it was probably due to a chemical imbalance, from which many women suffer after the birth of children. My emotional breakdown started a couple of months after my son was born. I became pregnant again almost immediately, and the depression was then postponed until after my daughter's birth.

A few months after she came into the world, I became so far inside myself that I couldn't be reached. I was a quiet sort of individual anyway, but now it had gone to the extreme. I could hear people talk to me and I could respond, but it didn't feel real. My husband was very good about trying to take me out and keep me entertained when he wasn't working, but he was as helpless as I as to what to do. I was under doctor's care, and was placed on a wonderful life-saving drug which kept me going, and eventually pulled me back into reality. From that time on, I developed an extremely high regard for medicine.

My doctor would only renew my prescription a set number of times until one day he said to me, "I will give you one more prescription, and I suggest you find out what is really bothering you so you can fix it."

I had thirty more days of security. After my extended maternity leave had ended, I was able to find a new job assignment at a location closer to my house and had returned to work. I carried the drugs with me daily, watching the clock carefully to take them on time. I was deathly afraid of depression, and these pills could miraculously bring a smile to my face within twenty minutes of taking one.

When I approached the end of the prescription, I dared save the last two pills for dire emergency. I carried them with me in a small pill bottle for so many years that they actually disintegrated, but I didn't need to take them.

Some years later, a doctor prescribed a derivative of the drug in a milder form as I had been experiencing several nervous symptoms. I had what I called "lock jaw," where my jaw became stiff, or my legs showed variations of discoloration due to stress, or the skin would wear off of the corner of the palms of my hands from being tense. Other times I had a burning sensation on my back, and burning behind my ears, and all those symptoms of a nervous person. Again, drugs became my salvation and carried me through to live a normal life.

Today, many years later, I have outgrown the need for such assistance. This is probably because I am not trying to juggle pleasing a husband, two children, taking care of a home and working. At one point in my life, with a failing marriage, I even managed to put myself through school at night to obtain a Master's degree. I did not do it without recourse, however, as I had the feeling that I had the flu every time there was an exam. It was only my nervous system acting up, but I would virtually be sick. But that's all over, now, and I am still working without all that stress and without the need for medical reliance.

CHAPTER THREE

As Friendships Go

In the early 1980's I had been laid off from Hometown Motors, the major concern for whom I had worked for many years. I had volunteered for the layoff as I had been forced into a job I did not want, and it seemed the only way out. I had been told that in order to get a transfer to another position, it was necessary to be out of work. If I was laid off, I could get called back to a new assignment.

I therefore volunteered. I probably would have been selected for layoff anyway, because the supervisor knew that I didn't want to be there, and he was forced to take me just as I was forced to take the assignment.

In my previous position with this major firm, I had been working on a project with an outside concern who hired volunteers. I called this Chamber of Commerce office and spoke to the President, Suzanne Lane. She was more than happy to set up an interview with me, which amounted to a free lunch.

We set up a schedule for me to work three days a week. That worked out fine for me. It got me out of the house three days a week, provided many contacts for job opportunities, and gave me two days to look for other employment. With the total of unemployment and unemployment benefits working out to be more than my normal pay, the money worked out fine, too. The only drawback was that it delayed my divorcing my husband, because I had no job security.

That is when I met Gwenn. She had at one time worked for the Council part time, but requiring more money, signed up with a temporary agency and got a full time job. Her assignment was just across the street from the Council, and for the company I had been layed off from, Hometown Motors. Because of its convenience, she still maintained a once-a-month assignment with the Council, taking Board Meeting minutes, and I would see her monthly on that day or if she just stopped in.

I had made friends with the secretary of the Council, Margie, who was about fourteen years younger than I. She was very friendly and had no apparent barrier to any age group. She socialized with friends and family members of all ages. She was also friends with Gwenn, and at a later date, Margie and Gwenn moved in together.

Margie was moving out on her own for the first time, and Gwenn had left her philandering husband. Gwenn's husband also had some business in the Council neighborhood, and perhaps with the Council, so I had met him and saw him when he occasionally came by. Gwenn and I were the same age.

Margie was a darling, young girl. She had a pretty face and a trim figure. Her personality was bubbly, and her nature welcoming. She loved to show off her young figure in front of the other members of the council (all female), and in some cases developed in them the jealously she had wanted to achieve.

Gwenn, on the other hand, was more masculine in her demeanor, and portrayed that she was extremely capable and could handle anything. She actually was quite bright and had the ability to do most anything that she put her mind to.

She dressed more staunchly, had a respectable, feminine build, and lovely long dark hair. In the next few years she had a couple of major surgeries close together, one of which was for breast cancer, and she began to gain weight. She was also told to cut her hair short for chemotherapy treatment, and at that point, surrendered the last of her real youthfulness. Life during this period had not been kind to her.

Occasionally Margie, Gwenn and I would do something after work together, but it was generally a Council public relations activity. While Gwenn was a very nice person, she was troubled with the breakup of her marriage. Because of my own unhappy state, I did not find myself particularly drawn to her. I found her to be an extremely capable person, and perhaps too stern and serious to be overly welcoming. Since I was in between divorce filings myself , neither of us needed to carry the other. Light-hearted Margie seemed to hold more attraction for both of us.

As time went on, however, and with Margie and Gwenn now sharing their second dwelling together, we all became friends. I, too, moved on my own after about the fourth divorce filing. (You would have to agree that with this many reconciliations, my ex-husband and I deserved credit for trying to make it work before finally breaking up the marriage. It actually took five filings before we managed to divorce.)

While this triad of Margie, Gwenn and myself continued for a few more years, Margie and I had a falling out. It was due to what I termed abnormal and unhealthy emotional behavior. Margie began creating phenomenal stories regarding her men friends and did many peculiar things to attract attention. When I brought the truth to her attention, the friendship ceased. The event of her behavior that brought our friendship to a crescendo was her taking revenge on an old boyfriend who had dumped her for another woman. She went as far as getting him back into her life, marrying him on a wonderfully romantic wedding in Hawaii, but never was true to him.

A year or so prior to getting married, Margie met a man at work, Dave, whom she really liked. Being too soon after his divorce, she was unable to convince him to marry her. The returned lover of a couple of years previous, and also holding high attraction, was willing to make that commitment, and they married. Joe was closer to my age, however, and the one who had dumped her a year prior. This marriage lasted all of three months when Margie, who had never stopped seeing Dave anyway, left the holy union.

She then managed to marry Dave in a similar fashion on a trip to Las Vegas. I am happy to report that I did see them together some years later and they appeared to be very happy. They just look like they belong together, too. I'm sure Dave is very good to her and he did seem to understand her idiosyncrasies before he married her.

For whatever reason, Margie sought to drop Gwenn as a friend when she dropped me, which left us open to develop a closer relationship. Gwenn, too, had grown tired of Margie's shenanigans and it became more and more difficult to ignore. We both tried to help her, but to no avail.

As far as our friendship went, admittedly, I was skeptical of Gwenn's then hyper nature. As the years went on, however, and she included me her circle of friends and other activities, I found her to be a delightful person. We have been friends, now, for about fifteen years.

CHAPTER FOUR

Sewing Club

One of the regular activities that Gwenn had involved me in was a sewing club that had formed many years ago. The girls were in their early teens when it was formed and some are still members today. It is almost unbelievable that this group, having many new members and some drops over the years, could still be meeting after more than thirty years. Gwenn calls it a sisterhood, since many of the girls have no sisters, and their conduct is such as to be supportive and understanding of one another.

During the first few years of this open invitation of monthly get togethers, I seemed to find more interesting things to do and did not go regularly. I was single, unstable, and young enough to be able to date during the week. At that time dating held more attraction than a room full of ladies.

As the years passed, however, my priorities have changed to be more in line with the other girls, who find this meeting almost as essential as breathing. There is something to this group of women who come from all walks of life and marital status. It is a union like none other that I have seen. The girls are not only fun to be with, but they seem to provide a necessary touch-stone and something special to each of us and for our well being.

In actuality, what was once strictly a club that did sewing, has evolved into any type of craft, but particularly those involving sewing. Many of the girls do quilting, ribbon embroidery, crocheting and knitting, but the list of crafts can include anything from painting to string art. Gwenn, in fact, makes jewelry and even likes to carve wood or soap stone.

The unwritten rule of the club is that it is not even necessary that you do some project when you meet. If you just want to unwind from the day's stress or just come for the camaraderie, that is perfectly acceptable.

Since I have been a member, some twelve or more years now, I haven't seen anyone drop from the club. We have added a few members, but basically the club stays the same. For the last four or five years now, we have even managed to travel as a group one or two times a year for extended weekend sewing ventures.

One of my former neighbors, who happens to be a Tarot card reader, introduced her boyfriend to our club members during one of her drop-in visits to my house. He asked, "How long have you girls been together in this club?"

Knowing that he had recently left a twenty-five year marriage, Gwenn responded, "Longer than your marriage lasted."

Over the life of the club, some of the girls' marital status have changed. During my tenure, there has been one divorce and one re-marriage. The nice thing is that it doesn't matter who is married and who is not. Sewing is the common ground. In regard to marital status, Gwenn says, "The men come; the men go; Sewing Club stays."

CHAPTER FIVE

My Two Children

During the years of struggle with divorce, the ones who suffered most, and my husband and I suffered plenty, were my two children, Doug and Sue. While it was not apparent to me at the time, they each felt unloved. Satisfying their own needs, they both got into trouble with drugs. They were pretty young to do that, but the times of society made drugs abundant, and they were able to buy them right on the school grounds.

It was quite a few years before I had any idea such a thing was going on, and I never could tell with my son while I was living in the marital home. Sue, however, showed signs of extreme "giggle" bouts that were not what I thought normal, only because I was looking for signs, and in later years saw that her eyes were as large as saucers. Because she and her friends seemed like quite normal children, it was very difficult to determine exactly what was going on. It is still amazing to me how you just can't always tell, even when they're your children and you're looking for it.

Nevertheless, they were now in their mid-teen years, Doug a year older than Sue. They were making it through school, and I was making it through living in and out of an unhappy marriage. I finally made a big break, bought a condominium on my own, and moved while my husband was out of town. It was a nasty thing to do, but I felt it was the only way. He had threatened on more than one occasion that if I divorced him, he would see to it that I got nothing, and I was afraid.

The move was made, but without moving my children with me. I had waited until they were both of driving age and each had cars to get to me on their own, and gave them each a key. They were very angry.

I had set up the one extra bedroom for either of them, and if they both chose to come and live with me, I had two extra beds and would set one up in my room for Sue. As it turned out, they each stayed with me at separate times, and neither for very long. Sue moved back and forth between her father and I, and when Doug came to live with me I immediately recognized he was using drugs, and when approached about it, he quickly removed himself from the premises.

Shortly after, Doug was picked up for possession of drugs with the intent to sell. With the help of his father, he was put on a work release program from jail after sentencing. His dad was operating a printing business at the time, and had the ability to work him several hours per day and on weekends to keep his time at the jail to a minimum. I was very grateful to his father for handling the situation so well. Doug was, too. In fact, it is a debt to his father I don't think he will ever feel can be repaid.

Sue was never picked up, but there were times I wish she would have been as a safeguard to keeping her alive.

How she lived through those years of "using" all hours of the night, and not coming home for days at a time, I'll never know. I do know, however, that there were times that she did not feel she would live through the night. It was on those nights that she would call me on the telephone and tell me about how much trouble her friend was in, and how worried she was about him. It was actually herself that she was talking about but didn't tell me, and thankfully, I never caught on. It saved me some grief.

Doug feels very remorseful about his experience, and hasn't fully recovered from feeling less worthy than others. I try to tell him that his experience was what society besieged on their age group, and that he wasn't totally to blame.

Sue, on the other hand, "my party girl," has remarked that she is glad she experienced what she did. Now that she is almost thirty years old, however, she feels that she lost ten years of her life. She regrets that she is still plodding her way through college when she feels she should have been done long ago.

The most absurd thing to me is that she tells me the reason she did drugs in the first place was because she couldn't get enough attention from her mother or father. I don't know any parents who could have been more attentive, then or now (I speak for myself, now, as she and her father no longer share a good relationship). What I have found, however, is that Sue not only requires my attention, she demands it. Even today, she is very commanding in her demeanor, and draws the attention of all around her. In hindsight, what seemed like a reality to her then was really only her perception. Her feeling of no one paying attention to her was not really neglect at all, just no the attention she required.

Obviously, the troubled marriage kept both children in turmoil for at least ten years when my husband and I tried over and over again to make the marriage work. Today, they are wonderful, healthy adults and have survived those troubled times. I honestly don't know how I would have done it any differently; therefore, I feel no guilt.

CHAPTER SIX

First Vision

For a long period I had only identified one vision, that of my daughter Sue. It was a spirit that entrapped her and kept her from freedom, growth, and peace of mind. She was a troubled girl, and her life was kept in turmoil. I have watched this object in my vision change its grip on her, allow her the freedom to walk in and out of its grasp, but never totally release her. For the past five years it has lessened in height and has provided her wide berth, but it does not go away. At least not yet.

This object looks much like an open trunk of a tree. When I first saw it, it totally embraced her, and she could not get out of it. It felt to me that this thing was an evil spirit that kept her confined and would not let her go. Its texture was not that of tree bark; however, its appearance did resemble it. Its surface was more smooth and wet, like that of a living substance of the sea.

It wasn't until I was having my artist draw some of the visions that I wanted to portray that she came up with what is probably my tree-like object. What she found was a picture of tree remnants that were part of a swampland. These particular trees are partially under water and are called mangroves. Further research tells me that the mangroves are low trees that grow in muddy swamps found on tropical coasts. They are adapted to

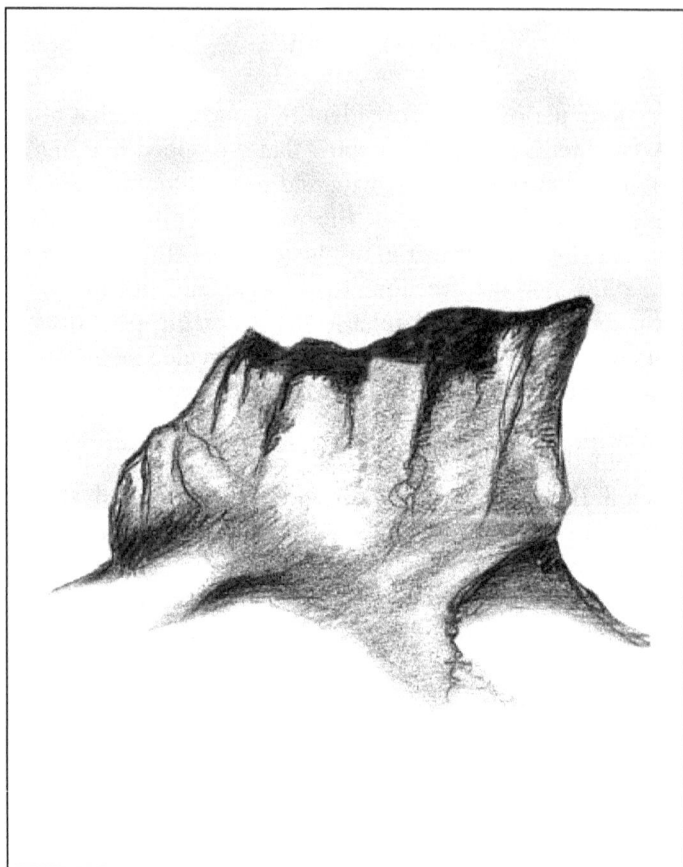

It appeared smooth and wet, like that
of a living substance of the sea.

live in creeks of salt water and they send down special breathing roots from their branches. Rare fish and a variety of animals live in the swamps where these trees grow. There appears to be many projects of replanting and preservation of these trees for the purpose of maintaining the marine ecological system.

Some years ago, I had gone to a psychic. I had been told that she could tell you things about someone by holding a piece of their jewelry, preferably gold or other metal. Although not metal, I handed her a string of black beads that I had worn, and which belonged to Sue. I was hoping she could give me some insight about my troubled daughter.

She held them in her hand and thoughtfully questioned, with a puzzled look on her face, "How old is your daughter?"

I told her she was 16. With some hesitation she stated, "Her soul is several years older than she, maybe 20 or 30 years--probably 20."

My mouth dropped open. I was stunned. I said, "Are we talking about reincarnation?"

"Yes," she replied.

Then I asked, "Is she reincarnated from someone in the family?"

"Yes," she said again. "Souls travel in family groups."

I do not know who this family member is, or if it is on my side or that of my former husband's. Since I have closely raised her, her training resembles my teachings. Her physical appearance, however, resembles her father's side. My guess is that this connected soul must have died about four or five years prior to Sue's birth.

Much to my dismay, the psychic explained that her life would go on like a roller coaster for four more years, at which time she would be 20. I felt that neither she nor I could make it that long if it did, but the roller coaster continued as she had said it would.

She told me that Sue was troubled because she was looking for the common thread that would unite her past life with her present, and until she found that, she would not have peace. She also explained that I could do nothing about it but be there for her, and I was and still am. This woman told me that her life would then settle out and that she would find happiness. And, she almost did for a brief interlude, which was the beginning of another struggle for her.

I left the meeting with the psychic totally in a maze of thought, and it took me several months to come to grips with this new information. As the years went on, and my daughter suffered still, the last of the four years began to show signs of relief, and some growth and direction for her life.

Sometime later, the vision of the tree-like substance appeared in my mind's eye. I mentioned it to Matt, a friend from a long-term relationship. Matt told me that some people were known to be able to see spirits of others.   I listened and remembered, but did no research on the matter. Sue would just have to live this one out, I presumed.

CHAPTER SEVEN

Immediate Family Spirits

My Mother

The next spirit identified was that of my late mother, whose relationship with me in later years was rather strained. I found her to be selfish and self-centered, especially when I could have used her support with my young children and later troubled marriage. Whether I saw her correctly or not I'm not sure, but the feeling was real, and so was the mental image.

My mother's spirit was that of a dragon. The dragon did not release venom or flames; however, her flashing words of the tongue were like emanating fire. There were times in my life that I considered her to be a shrew. Oddly enough, I learned by looking up the definition that a shrew can be a dragon.

That was not always true of her or of her disposition. She did have an occasional mean streak, but through her I learned to appreciate the goodness and kindness in human beings. I learned to forgive and forget, and to have compassion for the less fortunate. She taught me not to place judgment. She is the foundation on which I stand and I will love her and forever be grateful to her for it. But, an evil tongue she did have, and sometimes I pitied her for her lack of reasoning.

The flashing words of the tongue
were like emanating fire.

When she died, my stepdad said, to my utter amazement, "She will finally be rid of the demons that possessed her." He must have seen something similar to what I saw, but we never discussed it.

My Former Husband and Son

After our marriage was over, my former husband's life and style were filled with "trials and tribulations." On the business front, he was a poor manager and always spent over his limit on the dream that funds would be there to cover his expenditures. Bad practices and events led to the loss of the company and equity in the building. A re-established venture eventually resulted in the loss of the marital home, as he used it as a guarantee to cover his debts. One lawsuit followed another, for both he and my son, who has worked for and with him for many years now.

His spirit appears to me as a serpent, at the far end of a hot, bubbling, steamy pond. In the same pond, more toward the front, is my son. He is a friendly water snake who bobs up and down and swims freely in the warm, but not hot, water. As I think of it now, he is in the same pond as his father in real life matters, but I do not see him moving so freely. He is trapped, confined and controlled. I have been trying to communicate some words of wisdom for over a year now about breaking free of this "hold" that he feels is there, but with little to no progress. He works endless hours and countless days, without time off. His loyalty to his father and

31

A serpent is at the far end of a hot, bubbling,
steamy pond. More forward, a friendly water snake
swims freely in the warm, but not hot, water.

the business is so intense that he has given up his own life. He must feel a terrible debt so deep for his father's help and safeguarding during his childhood troublesome and difficult times. He is guilt ridden for the serious drug-related mistakes he made as a young man, for which his father graciously and intuitively handled for him. He must feel that the assistance from his father can never be repaid, for he has never taken control of his own life.

One day while looking through catalogs at my friend, Gwenn's house, I happened across an order book of catalogs. On the face of one catalog of dragons was a picture of my entire family! There was a dragon (my mother), perched on top of this tree-like trunk (my daughter), in the pond with the serpent (my husband), in the steamy background and the water snake (my son), in the foreground. It took a little imagination to see the steam I felt was there, but not much. I asked to cut the picture out, and carried it in my wallet for many months to come. I did not consider ordering the book at the time; however I have since regretted it. I tried to research it with the publisher but found that old copies are strangely not archived. I have also been watching for that picture that appeared on the front cover to re-appear in some catalog.

My negligence stemmed from disbelieving in the visions that I had seen, and not finding any relevance in what the book might contain. How foolish, now that I am more attuned to the fact that my family's spirits are all around "water," which I now reason has always been an attraction to me. Throughout my entire life, from

On the face of one catalog of dragons
was a picture of my entire family!

childhood on, I was enthralled by water. Today my home is located on the bay of a large lake. It is Lake St. Clair, and some call it the smallest of the great lakes.

I said to my friend, "Gwenn, my visions of the people I know are so often of things in water."

She replied, "Of course. They are all in the same family." She was referring to "soul family," of course.

CHAPTER EIGHT

The Meeting of Matt

It was within the first couple of years of returning to work after my son and daughter were born that I met Matt. He was working in the same building as I, but not the same department. I had seen him in the hallway a few times. I remember him suddenly appearing one day and making somewhat of a fool of himself for my attention, and I gave him a look which he later described as "get bent." "Get bent" was an old expression used by our age group in our late teens probably meaning to get lost. We were now in our early to mid-twenties. He took my cue, feeling stupid for his actions, and retracted back into one of the offices.

On one particular day, he and I were leaving work at the same time. While walking to our cars, he extended an invitation to me to have a coffee with him. I was complimented by the invitation, but declined as I had to get to school. I was attending the community college nearby. I also declined because we were both married and I certainly didn't know how to handle this. It was flattering, however.

Matt was a tall, nice looking, fair complected man. He had a wonderfully appealing personality, and was so gregarious and willing to please. He skillfully and naturally directed his conversation right into your interests. No wonder he later became a number one salesman with two major firms.

A short time later I heard some scuttle about Matt seeing another girl in the building. Well, I had suspected his invitation to me was because he was interested in an outside affair, and now, I thought, he has one. Some years passed, and somewhere along the line I transferred to another division and no longer worked near him.

I believe it was about ten years later, actually, after I had been voluntarily laid off from the company, that I was traveling past my old place of employment in my car. It must have been about quitting time and I was coming home from my volunteer job. I was headed for a drug store to pick up some vitamins.

When I approached the counter to pay for my selections, who should appear but Matt. He made small conversation, and I assumed he just happened to be in the same store at the same time. Little did I know then that he had seen me in traffic and had deliberately followed me into the store for the purpose of such a chance meeting.

This time he invited me to stop for a drink so we could finish our conversation. My marriage, at this time, had already gone one round of filing for divorce by my husband. The divorce was called off at the present time; and I was, after all, basically unemployed. I needed to be able to support myself before proceeding. I accepted, and this time agreed to give my telephone number where I could be reached during my three-day-a-week work schedule.

His calls to me were persistent and regular. His marriage was in no way ready to end, but he obviously was discontent with it and continued to seek other relationships. A divorce was somewhere in his distant plan, but he now had a four year old added to his older two boys to raise.

What began as a re-acquainted friendship, eventually turned into an affair. I actually had no serious interest in this man, but his company was good, his compliments flattering, and his attention much needed. It was not until several years later, because "he just didn't go away," that I developed a real love for him--when I learned how deep his heart and soul were with genuine feeling.

CHAPTER NINE

The Newest Family Member
and Soul Mate

The newest addition to my visual pond was Matt, my dear friend and lover of many years now, whom I saw as some type of water critter. With its head above water, holding on to a rough, flat board, it did nothing but observe. I dubbed this critter as a "bump on a log," as was true with Matt's character. I felt his life was stagnant. He did nothing meaningful with it nor did he make any strides to go forward. His placement in the pond was more forward than that of my son.

The way visions came to me was just to think of the person, and the image would appear in my mind's eye. Many times I would create an immediate "block," and see nothing. I would not want to see it. I did not really want to accept that there was any credence to what I mentally created in my mind.

I might also mention, that my life has been drug free during the entire time that I have observed these visions. I have not required any medical attention for nervous symptoms, so any thoughts of these "visions" being medically induced is unfounded!

Additional insight was given to me by an artistic acquaintance in regard to my "bump on a log." Whenever I related the elements of this vision to

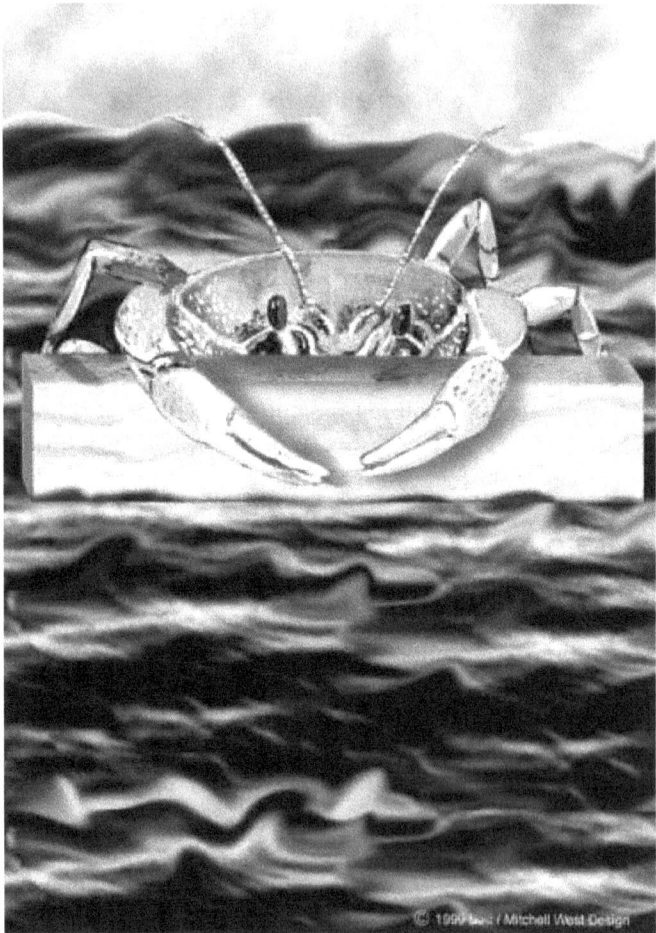

A "bump on a log."

someone, I would also note that the log was really never a log. This critter was balancing himself on a flat board.

"Isn't 'board' a condition of one's life," he queried? "And wasn't he just keeping his head above water?" There were two pieces of information given me that I had never considered. I am so short sighted with this gift. I must learn to be more insightful!

About nine months ago, now, after fourteen years, my dear friend, Matt, made a decision to take an intermission from me. He was unable to give clear explanation as to why this was needed. His statement was that he "felt compelled to do this." I did not ask why, as I knew the relationship had not gone well for the past few years. Nor did I ask how long he might be gone, or suggest that it might be forever--but that was a distinct possibility we both knew.

Since he had only been divorced for two years now, one might suspect that due to our long-term relationship that he was feeling the pains of needing to make a marriage commitment and that was not comfortable to him. Nor was it his desire at that point in time and probably what caused him such consternation the past few years we were together. To relieve himself of this internal pressure, he sought to take leave.

In the first year, fate made us cross paths a few times. The first time was three months after the break, when I found myself two car lengths behind him in traffic. I did not attempt to catch up with him. In fact, I turned off to avoid him.

Again we met, only face to face. I had come home from work very early that day, and he had some business with my next door neighbor and did not expect me to be home at that time. I was sitting outside at the back of the house when he arrived. He tried to make light conversation with me, but every word infuriated me more as it involved his life from which I had been removed.

I turned and went into the house, leaving him to stand there alone. He was not the person he use to be, not taking "no" for an answer. At one time he would reach to the bottom of his soul and divulge his feelings until there was an understanding between us. Now he said nothing and drove away, breaking my heart again.

The next time was two months later, just prior to his birthday. I pulled out of the parking lot from work, leaving early for a hair appointment. It was quite uncommon for me to leave early, and there I was, directly behind him in stopped traffic. I recognized the car ahead immediately, and he looked into his rearview mirror and spotted me as well.

I was more receptive to a chance meeting this time, and pulled ahead of him nodding hello as I passed. I had planned to make a stop to pick up a paper, and pulled into the parking lot. He followed, and if he would not have, I would have been devastated. I truly loved him and wanted to see him.

In conversation, he poured out everything that had gone on in his life since our separation, most of it troublesome. Two of his three boys had not progressed well in terms of secure jobs and certainly not careers. The third, youngest boy, had gotten into trouble too often and was needing close attention. Also, one of his sisters, presumably anorexic, was not doing well and refused family intervention and/or medical help. He said that his family had done all they knew to do, and had basically accepted that she was going to die.

He attempted to kiss me on the cheek and I pulled away, which he later rationalized was a natural reaction based on the circumstances. We said good-bye, but the conversation about his sister haunted me to the point of tears. I'm sure I was even more emotional about having seen him and that I did not have him. I knew he loved me but could not control or find a solution to his troubled mind about being confined to the relationship.

I talked to my daughter, and told her about seeing Matt and the sad situation of Matt's sister, Rachel. Sue reminded me that there was something that could be done based on her experience with an emotionally disturbed former mother-in-law. She told me that a family member could go to the court and have her petitioned to be picked up because she is emotionally disturbed and is refusing medical help. I then remembered that she and her husband-to-be did that with his mother to get her help when she refused.

I called Matt's car phone number and left him a message to that effect, saying that it was certainly a personal decision because the person whose life is affected may never forgive the action. However, it might save her life. My message ended with a long pause, and then, "Whatever happens, I love you."

That was not all that bothered me. I was totally emotional over Matt the following day, which was Friday. I talked to one of my closer friends at work, crying, and then called my dearest of friends, Gwenn, who immediately offered to accept me into her home for the weekend and coddle and spoil me.

I went to her home on Saturday, with barely a thing packed, not even a toothbrush. I literally dumped myself on her to take care of me. I could not understand why this man, who clearly loved me as much as I loved him, was unable to make things work for us. He was unable to make a commitment to me-- which he has refused to do, or to make me any part of his family life.

Through Gwenn's divine intuitiveness and assistance that weekend, I learned that Matt had "family debts" to pay, and with me in his life, he was unable to take care of his first responsibilities. His statements to me were of needing to put "closure to his life." He said he could not see me in his future, for he saw no future for himself. It was so sad to hear these words he felt so sure about.

For two days, Gwenn and I thrashed ideas back and forth, with me pouring out my heart on how I did not want to lose his love. And with enough input, probably on the first day, she was able to present to me a clear metaphor of what Matt's life was about at this time. I did accept this input, even if not fully understanding his current position in life. The second day I was still searching for understanding, as the answer was not settling well with me. By late afternoon of the second day, I am sure I had exhausted Gwenn's psychic powers, but had resolved to understand the following information which was presented to me this way:

Matt had a lot of over-extended credit cards. In his lifetime, he could only see the ability to pay on four of the five that he owned. He had one for each of his three boys, and one for his sister, for whom he had not been able to take responsibility. He lacked personal strength (a shared family trait wherein each was dysfunctional, and now recognized by Matt). No family member was able to do what was needed. The outstanding credit card that he could afford not to pay was for me. It was a debt he could let go.

Gwenn explained to me what she had learned from a very recent lecture at church about debts that people have, one of which was family debts. And that was exactly the debt from which Matt suffered. He had, over the years, spent much too much time with me at the expense of his family, and they were calling their debts due. Each of the boys told him in their own way that what he did (spending the time with me) was right for him at the time, they understood, but it was not right for them. And I did accept that he must repay those debts, and until they were paid, he could not be free.

Gwenn also explained that she was sure that he dearly loved me, but that he may never be able to repay those debts in this lifetime. She assured me, however, with knowingly little consolation, that Matt and I would "make it some day together," if not in this lifetime, perhaps the next. It gave me some solace, but little relief, for I ached with love for him. She also rationalized, if I could keep hovering until Matt was ready to have me land, we might make it yet—but it could be four years, ten years, or next lifetime.

Did I want to wait that long?

On the second day, one of the questions Gwenn asked me to think about in trying to understand Matt's standing in life was, "What is Matt's motivation in life? What makes him get up in the morning? What is he living for?" she asked.

The answer did not come immediately, but when it did, I knew. This was the answer to the question about his statement of needing to bring closure to his life. "Matt is living to find peace of mind," I said. "He can't go on in life until he finds peace of mind."

I thanked her graciously for her time and love that weekend; however I could never repay the peace of mind she gave me. We briefly talked about the talent of the young girl who had been my next door neighbor, and reader of Tarot cards, when she disclosed to me, "I feel I have a gift, too." And I have learned that she very much does.

With my new-found understanding, I told her I had to tell Matt that I now understood. After I got home and got settled, I called him at his home around 8:30 p.m. He was very receptive to my call. I explained my newfound knowledge about family debts, and he agreed. I explained that Gwenn had helped me to understand his position and that she had taken such good care of me in my delicate and battered condition. He said he would be forever beholding to her.

We talked about many things, all the things that we each had stored on similar lists of why the relationship had not worked, what things were wrong, and so on. We laughed, as we decided in reality they would not hold water, and those that did were because of the family debts he needed to pay. I was also able to enlighten him on his feeling of needing to put closure to his life, and he was astounded to learn that he had mislabeled his feelings and needed to find peace of mind. And, peace of mind was on his list of things that were needed in the relationship.

Two hours into the conversation, Matt was saying, "Don't go." Three hours into the conversation, he was telling his son, Alan, "This is Ellen, I'll be awhile." And we talked and laughed and loved for four and one-half hours on the telephone. And when we hung up, he called back to say he loved me, and we talked another half hour.

Gwenn tells me Matt's soul and my soul are connected, and that is why it is so painful for us to be separated.

CHAPTER TEN

The Good Old Days with Aunt Addie

When I was a little girl, my Aunt Addie always bought me the cutest things for my birthday and Christmas. She just had a knack for gift giving that was so suitable for a young lady growing up. She might buy me a particular kind of belt or an evening bag I was too young for, but loved. Once she bought me three colorful straw hats, in green, orange and yellow, which I saved forever. The hats were actually made of feathers, and when I wore them my children use to laugh and call me "Big Bird."

At Easter time she had egg dye which her two boys used to color their Easter eggs. I had visited with her for a day shortly before Easter one year, and she had saved the dye so I could color eggs at her house. It was one of those enjoyable childhood memories I will never forget. I don't know what made that day so special, because I certainly colored eggs at home and had a lot of fun doing it. Somehow, being able to do it there was really special.

Aside from occasional visits, I was not really that close with my aunt until the years after my divorce. It was then, after my children had grown up, that I had the time to spend with her. We had fun going to card readers once in a while or just taking rides and going to dinner. We also loved going to garage sales, a real favorite pastime. One time, shortly after I moved into my current home, we planned to have a garage sale ourselves. We accumulated so much stuff for this event that we had to keep the sale going for three weeks in order to unload it! We still donated a truckload to a worthy service.

Whenever I had parties at my house I always invited her so that she would have fun too. She was wonderful to have around, and she helped clean up after my other guests before I could get to it. Sometimes I would feel guilty because she worked so hard when she was there, but she loved to do it and seemed to really enjoy herself.

She was such a cute little petite lady with her curly, dark hair and light complexion glowing. She had such a good nature that she was always willing to do whatever I wanted to do, let me take her home whenever I was ready (she didn't drive), or she would stay the night if I got too tired when evening came.

I ached for her when I first began to see signs of dementia and her not being able to care for herself. Now that she is in a home for Alzheimer's patients, I see her as often as I can, bring clothing to her, and take her out for the afternoon or evening.

CHAPTER ELEVEN

Spiritual Visions of Family, Friends and Associates

Aunt Addie

Getting visions of other family members and friends was becoming more common. Sometimes I blocked them, and sometimes they changed over time. They occasionally just happened; I just didn't invite or welcome them.

My Aunt Addie, was at one time visualized as a plain, white tablecloth. I never tried to rationalize what that meant, I just accepted it. She later became "spring flowers of the most brilliant colors, illuminating in the brightest light." I somehow feel it was her place in heaven. She is not there yet, but you might say she is close. Now, with Alzheimer's disease, her entire life is present with her from beginning to now as if it were all happening at once.

I sometimes feel that she is more with it than the rest of us as she is not hampered with the constraint of time.

When she was an active, more mobile individual, she and I would go to a clairvoyant reader from time to time. She enjoyed that. After the first one we saw, we exchanged stories the next day of the strange occurrences that happened to each of us for our unapproved journey into the future. I complained that I kept walking into things in my house, banging up my legs, and she claimed that a clock "jumped" off of her wall. We laughed, but were skeptical of the strange happenings. That was the time the psychic told me that my daughter was a reincarnation of an earlier soul.

Another time she explained to me that she had visitors during the night. They were ghosts. One was her late husband, and the other was a woman with dark hair that she did not know. Her jealousy of her husband with another woman prevailed, having brought forward a memory of someone who may have had an affair with her husband when he was still alive.

Matt wondered if the lady was really her as a young girl, and that she did not recognize herself. They ghosts stood in her bedroom, facing the wall, but said nothing. Aunt Addie had awakened to go to the bathroom. She acknowledged their presence, took care of business, and went back to bed. I believed her.

Aunt Addie was a heart patient, having had a by-pass some years back. Her heart had stopped at one point recently and she had been revived. I thought about the ghost story and felt at that time that her husband had come to take her, but she wasn't ready to go. She had such a lot of vigor and spirit.

My Friend, Gwenn

Gwenn, at one time, presented herself to me in the form of a perfectly square box having crisp corners. This was an all too true symbolism of her life. She is extremely "black and white," or "cut and dry," in her thinking and very being, so the box fit her well. That was before I learned of her true depth and ability to transverse beyond normal, limited thinking.

Later, her image transformed into the prettiest little glittering, sparkling angel, as she went on about her work with her magical wand, spreading good tide to all things she touched. She was so happy, flitting from place to place, as she is when she is helping people. Her image remained a sparkling angel for some time, until one day I noticed that it wasn't sparkling any more. She was unhappy at work, and it was showing.

This same angel has taken on a new look from time to time as I take readings, but has never glistened as it did when I first saw it. When she is sick, it takes on a gray shadow. I asked her one day, "Gwenn, where have you been? You are all covered with soot!," to find that she had bronchitis. And another time, since she no longer sparkles (problems still at work), I found her with the prettiest, guilded wings of gold and a painted face, when normally she wears the modest of clothing and makeup. When I queried her about this attire, she explained it was in her new attitude. She was going to go to work and not let on how she was feeling inside, but she would act and dress the part of a happy person, loving her job. That worked for a short time.

And so it is. The visions change with what is going on in life. Her latest image is of no more felonious glamour, but of a simple white, short, angelic dress, perhaps of eyelet, and she is moving carefully and carrying her wand. The wand resembles a Tinkertoy (dowel rod and round wheel), or perhaps a mallet used to play the xylophone. I wish she would again find the happiness that made her glitter.

Delphine

One night while sitting at the bar of a popular restaurant and evening mingle place with my daughter, a young little sex pot came in with her apparent boyfriend. The little sex pot was very friendly, and began a conversation with me. She wore a short, black leather skirt and a black leather vest that zipped up the center just below her bra line, exposing her black bra. Quite obviously, she was dressed for the attention. I later found, when she did not get it, she went after it.

Why she made identification with me I did not immediately understand; however, I was needed in her scheme of things to come. I enjoyed her friendliness, and my daughter seemed to ignore the situation, but was, I am sure, aware. Her name was Delphine, and she claimed that her boyfriend didn't care what she did— whatever that was supposed to mean.

As the music played, Delphine and the boyfriend did not get up to dance, but she asked me if I would dance with her. My daughter and I had not attracted any male counterparts, just lookers, and even though I don't normally dance with another female, agreed to do so. I was probably somewhat pleased that a young person found me pleasant, and she was not threatening to me, even in her attire.

Moments after reaching the dance floor, I found her dancing to attract the attention of onlooking men. She was friendly, and pulled one onto the floor to dance with us, just having fun. The song ended, and we each returned to our respective spots at the bar.

I'm sure at some point she introduced herself to my daughter, Sue, who was nonplused with meeting her acquaintance. I'm not sure why I was so tolerant.

Delphine asked if I would dance with her again, and being relatively unentertained with the events of the evening I again agreed. When we reached the dance floor, Delphine began going after men, explaining to me in some terms as to how she enjoyed their reactions to her, and her power. She not only threw herself at onlooking men, but now she was outwardly going after men on the dance floor who were dancing with other women.

At the first recognition of this, I left her on the dance floor, and rejoined my daughter. Sue explained that she had seen an old flame there, and he had invited us to join he and his friends in an adjoining bar of the restaurant. We did, as I was anxious to part from

Delphine, and I knew Sue would be only too glad to rekindle a relationship with Ed.

Ed looked as great as ever, and welcomed me with his warm personality. I met one of his other two friends

A featherless, newborn, peeping bird, looking up at
Its mother hungrily, wanting to be loved and fed.
who had accompanied him, and we socialized until we
were invited to take a boat ride with them. The boat did
not belong to Ed, although he was its master that
evening, and it was docked right outside the restaurant.

Sue and I boarded along with Ed and Chester. Within
moments of starting the engine, the third party arrived
with guess who, Delphine!

"Delphine," I exclaimed!

Ed asked, "You know her?"

"Yes," I said. "I met her earlier in the bar."

I don't recall the fellow's name that brought her on
board, or if I even knew it. We started out into the lake
on our way out to a cove behind the Ford Mansion. It
was an area very protected with trees, and other boats in
the cove were some distance away.

Delphine somehow had attracted Ed enough that the two
of them jumped into the water, and I assume completed
some intimate maneuvers to my daughter's dismay and
disgust. The second person to become familiar with
Delphine was Chester, in what appeared to be some
necking and petting in the cabin below.

Shortly thereafter, we were pulling out of the cove, and
were on our way back to the restaurant. The fellow who

brought her on board now found a blanket to cover both he and Delphine. She then willingly lost her clothing and proceeded to complete intercourse under the covers on the back deck in the presence of all others on board. The boat docked, and Sue and I walked off, not saying even a goodbye. There was nothing to say; we were just glad that we arrived back on land safely. That ended any interest my daughter may have had for Ed. Done. She was totally appalled by his behavior.

The whole next day, and for several weeks to come, the image of Delphine and the remembrance of her scratchy, gruff but squeaky voice haunted me. I heard her voice over and over again, as I still can today, several months later. What I saw and heard then, and now, was a newborn, featherless, peeping bird, looking up at its mother hungrily, wanting to be loved and fed. It was obvious to me that she had received neither love nor food, and had thus become a whore, trying to get fulfilled. Delphine, her image and her voice, did not leave my mind for some time later.

Gwenn's Former Husband, Bob

Since I was getting visions more frequently, and discussing them with Gwenn, she asked me if I could see a vision of her former husband, Bob. Something tried to come forth in my mind, and I blocked it. I didn't want to know, as I had done with other visions in the past. She asked why I blocked it, and if it was because of my association with her. I told her I didn't know; I just didn't want to find out what his vision was.

A day or two later, I thought about Bob's vision, and I saw it. I didn't know what it was, but it was pretty clear in my mind, complete with color. I explained to Gwenn that I had seen it, but I didn't know what it was. I told her that I could draw it, but that I didn't recognize it. I described it as having made a fan-shaped, gliding landing, but I had no idea what it was.

We met for dinner, and on a table napkin I began to draw out this fan-shaped form, describing it. She started to throw out ideas, but I was rejecting them. Whatever she suggested I can't recall, but I explained, "Its surface is not right. This thing has a texture of something wet, like 'liver,' and its color is a very rich brown."

She asked, "Is it a Manta Ray?"

I said, "What's a Manta Ray?"

"A fish, with a wide fan-like spread, that is very graceful in the water."

I went home and looked it up in the dictionary. It described it as she had said, calling it a "devil fish," for it covered its prey like a blanket. I rationalized that it fit Bob's personality, for he very much appeared to take all under his wings--or at least wanted to feel that he could. He also captured many, encapsulating them with his gracefulness and charm as if under a blanket. I was sure she had defined what I could see.

A Manta Ray

My Friend, Nancy

Now that I was learning not to block visions as they came into being, I began playing with asking for them. I had talked to my friend, Nancy, at lunch one day. I shared a small sampling of the encounters I was having with visions, not knowing if she would or could believe in the experiences. She did not let on if she thought I was strange, but went along by asking if I could get a spiritual vision of her. I said I did not know. But when I tried at a later time, what I saw of Nancy was this.

The first vision was of thick lips of a person's face. Exaggerated lips. The second vision followed almost immediately. It was of an animal, like a duck or goose, with an extremely long beak. Both things that I saw were enlarged and exaggerated. The next time that I checked for Nancy's vision, I got a flock of fluttering geese. I could hear their wings flutter as they moved about the yard, but I'm not sure if I heard what other noises they made. I may have heard squawking, or it may be something I have added to the vision. There are times I cannot be sure.

The exaggeration I understand as a part of Nancy's character, for she overextends herself, mostly at shopping. It is the only real flaw I think she has. She is an extremely attractive lady, holding her age wonderfully. She wears clothing extremely well, so it is no wonder she likes to buy them. It is no surprise to see Nancy dressed all new from head to toe, each time you see her.

Generally, when one member of a family has an excessive trait, another member also has some disturbance in another form. I believe that is where Nancy's excessive nature comes from.

Nancy has two fine brothers, but one has not actually been able to live a normal life. He has had the misfortune of being addicted to alcohol, and is now a recovered alcoholic. His new addition is AA, a better choice, I'm sure.

He has been unable to become a real part of society. He works part time, is very bright, but spends every day of his life in AA meetings. A more recent report is that one of his inventions has taken off well and he has managed to launch some business from it. If this family association accounts for her extravagant spending behavior, she certainly cannot be blamed for an inherited trait.

The fluttering of wings, well, maybe it represents her dissatisfaction with her place in life. Perhaps she feels trapped in the yard, unable to get out of the reigns that hold her. Maybe she feels captive to a spending habit. I see no fence holding her, so she is trapped by her own volition.

My Cousin, Cheryl and One Daughter

When I asked for a vision of my cousin ,Cheryl, I got it. To my astonishment, I saw a dancing skeleton, much like that of a marionette, with strings. Why? I hadn't

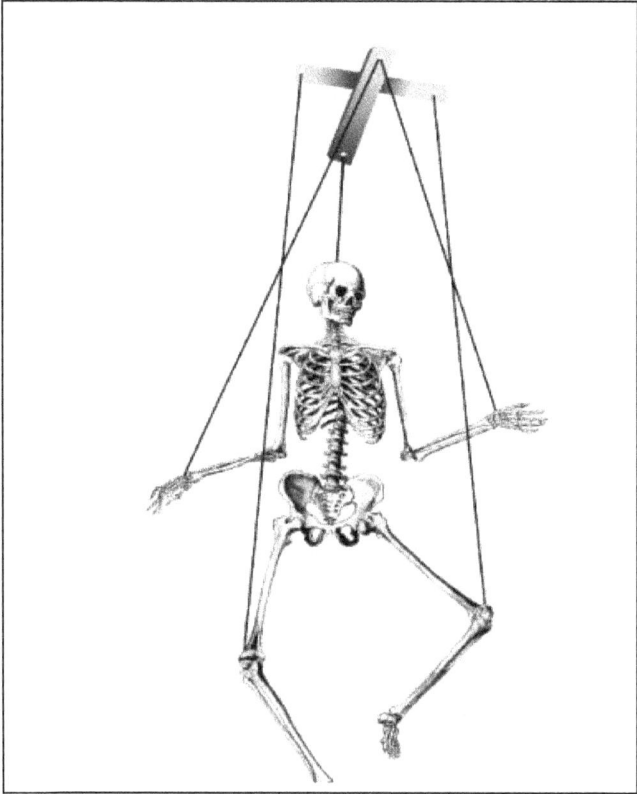

A dancing skeleton, much like that of a marionette.

A clue. It would be some time before I would discover what this symbolism meant.

She had explained to me one time that years prior she had gone to a psychic with a few friends. She had been the only one in the group who was told that she had been reincarnated. That spooked her, too, much like the information I received about Sue. After telling me this story over dinner one evening, she showed me her hands. The psychic had shown her how she had two distinct sets of prints in her hands, representing the current and previous life. I've not looked at Sue's, but shall make a point of it soon. I took a careful look at my own hands, and they did not reflect what I saw in hers.

When telling my artist acquaintance about this marionette, he asked me to describe it to him as if he knew nothing about a skeletal structure.

I said, "Well, it's hard, its parts are connected, and it moves freely. Its body is hollow, and in human form it is covered with flesh."

"There, you see," he said, "you have told me so much about this person, and you probably didn't even know it. This person is hard, is able to move freely, and much of her internal self is exposed."

Again I had to concede that I had not looked at the vision deeply enough. He had provided me with a valuable tool in which to better understand what I could see.

Cheryl has four children, one son and three daughters. For whatever reason, I thought about one of her daughters in terms of her spirit, and saw jaws--just

66

skeletal jaws. I was not able to conclude an interpretation for any of this, and Gwenn was not able to offer any insight when I shared the skeleton puppet with her.

Several months after having seen the vision, and after many times questioning its meaning, I have finally drawn my conclusion. Today, I interpret Cheryl's life to be entirely controlled by her predecessor, the soul from whom she was made.

She will probably return to life again as another being, for another trial, to overcome the strength of her other part. This time she has failed. Her daughter, Shelly, the jaws, is also a related reincarnated soul to her mother, whose thinking is expressed through the words from her mouth. Her words could be cutting, as were my own mother's, and are probably overly defensive in behalf of her mother's needs. There is much love between my cousin and her children.

In talking with Cheryl at a later date, she shared with me that she had recently been told by a psychic that her purpose in life was to learn "independence." She has no idea how strong she must become to break the strings of the marionette.

Rob, Sue's Late Husband

My daughter, Sue, had married about a year and a half ago. Within the first few months of marriage, her husband became deeply troubled and overwhelmed with the responsibility of the marriage, new home and life. He committed suicide four months after the marriage, leaving unanswered questions in the minds of family and friends, and other circumstances in disaster. The respite of happiness my daughter fought so hard for soon vanished.

Approaching the one-year mark of his death, at Gwenn's suggestion, I decided to take a reading of Rob. His vision appeared as a ghost. I was humored to see that Rob was a ghost! Of course he was a ghost, I thought. But the image of the ghost had its peculiarities. The face was elongated, as was the body. And the body was wavy, something I had never seen in any picture or representation of any ghost, so it had its own remarkable identification.

I thought about this ghost many times. Then one day, while shopping with a few girls from the Sewing Club, a very strange thing happened. I was browsing through the art section of a store, and the first picture in a stack on a shelf was of something very much resembling Rob's ghost. Its face was elongated, and its body was wavy. It was enough to make me shudder.

That same day, at another store, I was again drawn to the pictures. I didn't need any, so I don't know why I was

looking. Again, a stack of large pictures were in a box on the floor suitable for flipping through; and somewhere in that stack was the same picture, and the first and only one within that stack that I pulled out to view. It was Rob's ghost!

To add to the peculiar events of the day, another extraordinary incident happened. While still in that store with my friends, each of us browsing on our own, I was suddenly plagued with an alarming ringing, buzzing, sound in my ears and in my head. It was indescribable and enough to stop me dead in my tracks and wait until it was over. I was immobilized.

It lasted for maybe 15 to 20 seconds, and then went away. If you have seen the story that Annette Funicello made as her last movie of her life, you would know what I heard. The movie was regarding her learning of and living with multiple sclerosis, and depicted the sounds she had experienced which led to her diagnosis. I was too freighted to tell Gwenn that same day, but confided in her in a subsequent conversation how afraid it had made me to think that I may have had a first sign of MS.

Just before being seated for dinner that day with all of the girls, I was able to tell Gwenn, privately, about the pictures that I had seen. I described the extraordinary shapes and colors that I had seen, and remarked about their having been the likeness of "Rob's ghost."

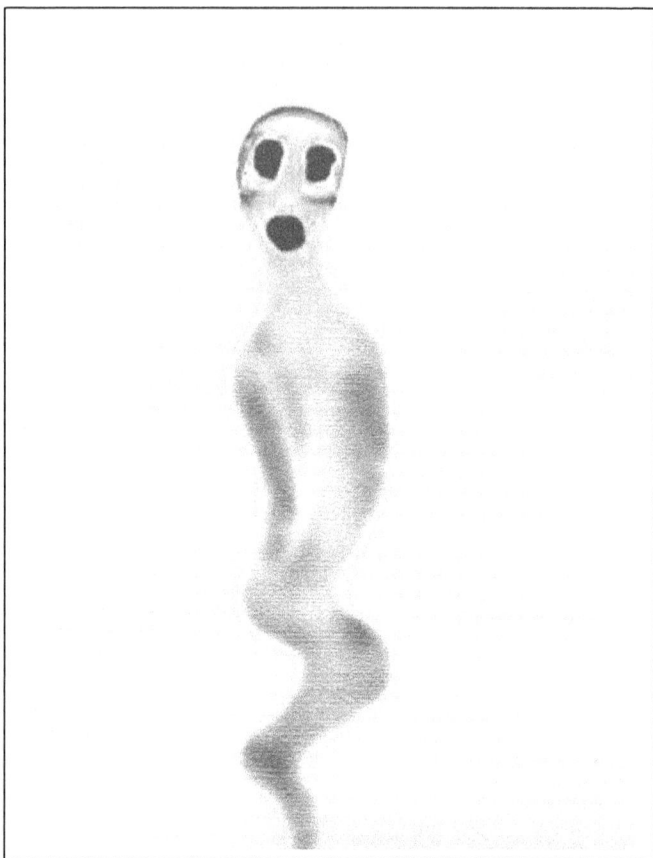

The ghost had a face that was
elongated, and the body was wavy.

She had already been given my description of Rob's
ghost. "Yes, she said.   That is 'The Scream,' a picture
to show how the artist felt when he was having his

nervous breakdown." I later learned that the artist's name was Edvard Munch. He was a middle-class, Norwegian artist.

From what I learned from a book I took out at the Library, Edvard was a troubled soul. He had experienced the loss of several family members in his young life, which is thought to have affected his mental state. He lost his mother at age 5, a sister at age 14, and his father when he was 26.

> While he became successful in his work, traveling to Switzerland, Copenhagen, New York and Berlin, his work depicted his inner despair. His frequent moves were thought to avert attention from his troubled state of mind.

> Much of his earlier work portrayed 'a piercing outcry' of his anxiety. *The Scream,* created when he was about thirty, was said to have evoked the 'feeling of a scream passing through nature itself . . . The terror-stricken victim is overcome by the realization of an unspeakable terror from within.'

> Edvard Munch entered a sanatorium for help in 1899, and later suffered a nervous breakdown in his fifties. His work at that time showed an 'emotionally diminished art in which a

degree of detachment and resignation takes place. . .'

I had not remembered then, but recalled something later that day when telling Gwenn about the pictures that I had seen. What I had recalled was that Brenda, the girl who reads Tarot cards, had told me that I would learn later that year something that Rob wanted me to know. It was something that he felt only I would understand. Also, when Brenda read Gwenn's cards she told her that Rob would be trying to communicate with her.

That was my message. I was sure. Chills and goose bumps ran through my entire body. Rob wanted me to know that he was having a nervous breakdown, that he was experiencing that terror from within, and that is why he ended his life. With his mother being ill for most of her adult years as a manic depressive, her years of living in and out of hospitals was not a life he would choose for himself and Sue. So he chose to end it. He also knew that I had had a nervous breakdown after my children were born, and I would understand how he felt.

Rob's communication with Gwenn was probably in her being able to give explanation to me. I would have completely missed the point of the pictures without her. That is why the communication happened the day when we were together.

The noise in my ears happened again the next day. It happened while I was at home, but for just a brief five seconds. And again it plagued me a few days later, but for only an instant.

Gwenn asked me if I was going to go to the doctor after the first reporting. I said if it happened again, I probably would, but I was not so sure it wasn't Rob sending me a message. I rationalized that the next two occurrences may have been more of the same type of communication from Rob, so I have discarded the incidents as being medically induced at this time.

Gwenn later told me that she had read that this noise that I heard in my ears has been heard by others who were being contacted by someone who had passed on. I was enchanted to feel that I had been chosen to receive such a communication, and relieved that this might be so.

In watching Rob's ghost over time in my vision, it has changed. As it drew nearer to the anniversary day of his death, at which time I feel he was trying to finally lay himself down in peace, I saw him struggling to get out of his ghost-like being. He was trying to be rid of it. As the time got closer, he ended up with the garb hanging around his ankles, but he was unable to get it off over his shoes. After some struggle, he just sat with it still at his feet, and appeared to give up, out of strength. Gwenn's perception was that Sue was not letting go of him.

After this anniversary date, I took further readings. He was now lying down on his stomach, head turned to one side, with one eye open. He was trying to sleep, but something would not allow him to rest. Gwenn, again, eluded to Sue's hanging on, and that she was punishing him. That vision stayed for about a month.

Then one day I began to see two, alternating visions. One was pathetic to look at, as Rob was being strangled around the neck and was bleeding, not the way he had died. He had died of a self-inflicted gun shot to his forehead. But he was suffering, now, as I am sure my daughter was. She was still very angry with him for leaving her, and obviously wanted to make him pay for her pain.

The next vision saw him dressed in a soft blue plaid flannel shirt, sitting on some steps. I have to struggle to remember the expression on his face. It is somewhat somber, maybe worried, sullen, empty, but complaisant. Maybe he was taking his punishment and contemplating the current state of his soul.

I hope for his sake and Sue's that they find a peace soon, so Rob can lay down to a final resting and she can go on with her life. She is returning to counseling now for some assistance in dealing with Rob's death. This is a wise decision.

Gwenn's Friend of Long Ago, Derek

I was now actively looking for visions whenever the thought occurred to me. Upon leaving Gwenn's house one evening, having had a discussion about her friend, Derek, I experimented with seeking a visionary spirit of him, someone I had never met.

I called Gwenn the next day and exclaimed, "Salt and pepper, in shakers!" A mental telepathy went into play, and she described the exact set of glass, tapered, silver-topped salt and pepper shaker set I had seen. We thought that pretty amazing but were unable to draw any conclusion as to what it meant.

A couple of days later, I was able to explain that the salt was his current wife, and the pepper was Derek. In my vision they were doing the soft shoe, and then the wedding dance. Admittedly this description of spiritual imaging has begun to sound far fetched, but I have since found God's humor in some of the visual pictorials I have received. It is what I saw, no matter how bizarre.

"Soft shoe, wedding dance; soft shoe, wedding dance." Gwenn felt the vision had its merits.

Derek and his wife were no longer engaged in a good marriage; in fact, it was about ready to explode. The soft shoe was the delicacy in which they approached living under the same roof at a time shortly before the holidays, and the wedding dance was the effort made to hold on to the marriage.

Myself

Since I was getting pretty good at allowing visions to appear without blocking them, and also bravely asking for them as well, I decided to find out if I could see my own spiritual vision. And I could. I appeared to myself as a young woman, probably younger than I am now. I had dark, medium-length hair, and I was standing at the top of a hill, with the breeze gently blowing the long, sheer, white-flowing dress that I was wearing. Am I at the top of the hill overlooking all that I see?

Was I overlooking all there was to see?

My Grandparents, Mother's Side

Upon the death of my mother, I inherited many of her personal belongings--home furnishings, dishes, clothing and jewelry. None of these things had real value, just personal value to me. Among the pieces of jewelry was a rhinestone cat's head with emerald green eyes. Piercing, green eyes. It was distinctly costume jewelry, but had an eerie look about it. Matt took one look at it, turned it face down in the box and put a rosary in with it before replacing its cover. It made him shudder.

Eight years later, I remembered how I always felt there was a reincarnation of a cat somewhere in the family. Today, I feel it is not an incarnation at all, but it may be an evil or mean and guiding spirit. It is with my late grandmother--someone with whom I always identified and cherished.

Then one day recently I asked to see a vision of my Grandmother's spirit, and saw the hissing, hunched-back cat. I told Gwenn of this discovery, and she said, "Ask her what her purpose is."

"Ask my Grandmother?" I said.

"Yes. She is the only one that can answer that. Ask her."

So I did, in one of my sleepy states, and got a faint and unclear answer. I think it had something to do with power," I told Gwenn when she asked me. I explained that it had not been real clear due to my sleepy state.

My answer sparked the statement, "Then the spirit is still there and hasn't been dealt with. I wonder what she wants."

"The spirit's attack is not with me," I said. "Our relationship was fine. The problem was with the relationship with her and my mother."

Gwenn's response was, "Then there are two (evil) spirits that have not been dealt with."

My grandfather's spirit, and probably not blood related to me, was that of a bull frog. "Mebeep. Mebeep. Mebeep."

That was about the right picture, too. He sat on the sideline with big, bulging eyes, and uttered only a comment or two.

Mebeep. Mebeep.

CHAPTER TWELVE

Visual Imagery Expounds

My Friend, Jon

If there ever was a gorgeous guy, it was my dear friend Jon, a co-worker for many years. I use to hope he would notice me every time he was anywhere near my office, but I never let on. He was not approachable, appeared unfriendly and certainly disinterested.

Rumor had it that he had married a girl while on a long-term assignment in Mexico. Supposedly, he never got over her, despite the fact that he was here in the states now without her. It is true that he did take every opportunity to work assignments that would send him back to Mexico. He looked for those liaison jobs. As with any work experience, once you have "Mexico" on your resume, you can be pretty well assured you will have first consideration when another such travel opening occurs. Besides, not everyone wants to travel there or take a chance of being assigned out of the country for any lengthy period of time.

During the days of our first working in the same office area, I would position myself so as to get in his way, or be in a place where he would have to walk around me. When his office was moved to the floor above me, twice I took an opportunity to walk up to his area to see if by chance he would just notice me. He never did. Or, he appeared to never notice me.

One day, several years later, we met by some destiny at an after- work pub. He was both friendly and cordial, much to my surprise. True, he had probably had a few drinks by then, but opened up to say that he had always admired me and would like to give me a call.

Well, he took my phone number, but he didn't call. He called a distant female acquaintance of mine instead, a friend he had seen socially in the past.

It wasn't until several years later, after he returned from a long-term assignment in Texas, that he and I met up again. This time he did call, and we met a few times for a drink after work.

Our first meeting was wonderful. Our conversation never lapsed, and we both talked so openly about everything. I felt he was someone I could really get close to. He spoke right from his heart—a rare quality—-and one I had only experienced once before, in Matt.

He ended the first evening with some hasty departing comment. I found it disappointing and strange, but accepted it. At the next meeting, he again found reason to break off at a given point in the evening. Again, I found it disappointing and peculiar.

By the next time I saw him, I realized what was calling him home. He was completely inebriated to start, drinking double Absolutes. His condition had deteriorated each time that I saw him, until I asked if it was drugs, alcohol, or both.

"It's alcohol," he replied.

Since we were able to converse well, we had a discussion on the "downward spiral" he was in. I told him that no good could come from his behavior. He listened and acknowledged, but admitted he had no desire to change his habits at this time.

Of course I knew, if the desire was not there, it wouldn't happen. We parted friends. He would call me sporadically, but more often I would call to check on him.

You see, I could see a vision of his state in my mind's eye. I could see him as a young boy of about eight or nine years old, standing at the end of a road. He had his thumb in his mouth and dragged a blanket at his side. I could see his need for nurturing and security. He was all alone.

The first time we met for a drink, he told me that he had been adopted as a small child. He also spoke of having a brother who had committed suicide. He stated that because he was adopted, he always felt like he didn't belong to that family. It didn't seem to matter that they loved him.

He also spoke of being a Godparent to a child in Mexico, and how he would make a special effort to go back to see the child. It was some time later that I reasoned that the child was actually his. He just didn't want to relate that he had a child of his own, and probably that he wasn't there to care for him.

Last year the child came to the States and visited him. I learned this in a conversation I had with him on the telephone. It was then that I asked if the child was his, but he denied that he was. He sounded pretty factual, but I doubted that this was not his child. I cannot be sure. If he were his child, and they were separated by countries, that may well be added reason for his alcoholism.

The Empty Tuba

Several years ago now, while working for Hometown Motors, a temporary girl had been hired into the office. She had the most delightful personality. I was drawn to her charming stories and humor. We became friends, and since we were both married, we occasionally did things as couples.

Patty was always very cheery, and a very talkative person. Thus, she was nicknamed "Chatty Patty." Whenever you called her on the telephone, she would answer hello, find out who you were, and begin talking. Sometimes I would talk to her at great length before I ever got to say what I called for.

I probably worked with her for many years before we each left the confines of the work environment where we met. We each made other friends along the way, and our friendship unfortunately waned after my divorce took place.

We were both "only" children, and thus had small families. She did not have any offspring from either of her two marriages. She is very close to her husband and is quite dependent on him, particularly for protection from anything she does not want to do or be a part of. It is easy to recognize when she uses him as a shield.

We still have conversations, rather infrequently, and meet for a meal once in a great while. As with all of us, she has a quirk or two, but one in particular is with money. At this time in our lives, with an upper middle-class lifestyle, I find it peculiar to grapple over a fifteen cent variation when splitting our bill. For whatever reason, this is important to her, when I know her home is paid for and she probably doesn't even need to work. Understanding people in general, I am left to reason that she is insecure about money, and is therefore very careful about its use. I am also quite certain that she is totally unaware of her behavior and means to offer no offense by it.

In one of our face-to-face conversations over dinner, holding back tears, she entrusted me with her frightful thoughts that when she died, no one would come to her funeral. She felt no one would be there for her. While she was normally so happy-go-lucky and had so many friends, she had such deep and empty emotion penned up inside her.

Sure enough. When I took the time to look at her spiritual vision, I saw a big tuba, sounding as deep and hollow as could be. How empty and along she must feel inside.

Her dad passed away within the last few years, and he was the parent with whom she most identified. She always had an interesting story to tell about him, and many times referred to some old adage that he had passed along her way.

The relationship with her mother had been more strained. She often worried that her mother would be very lost without her dad if her dad should decease first. She was sure that her mother would become terribly burdensome to her if this should happen.

In actuality, upon the death of her father, Patty's mom became a totally independent, fun-loving woman. She not only was not a burden to Patty, her pace of activities became difficult to keep up with. Now she and Patty have a good relationship, and enjoy the mother-to-daughter conversations that should have taken place many years ago. Patty, too, with this subconscious tension lifted, is lighter hearted and full of admiration for her mom. I don't think her tuba is quite as empty as it once had been.

Patty, incidentally, is one of those "messengers" from heaven for me. Every time I meet with her, I gain some insight into life that I had not known before, or am able to look at the next plateau I am to reach with greater knowledge.

For instance, the last time we met, she had much to say about her current relationship with her mom. In that she commented on how absurd her mom's conversation with her lady friends had sounded to her, and likewise, how strange our conversation would sound to the younger generation had they been listening. Her point was that we, too, would be moving into that same realm as we continued to age, and to be ready to accept those changes as they occurred. I always walk away with some new wisdom, and it is generally in a forward looking mode.

She claims that I enlighten her in much the same way each time we meet.

Space Cadet

Jill, one of my sewing club friends, is a very sweet lady. She never forgets to do something I ask of her or to remember me when she comes upon something she thinks I might like. She is quite content with her conservative life of baby-sitting for her niece and nephew or for the children of a man with whom she had worked. Her other pastime is, of course, sewing.

She never expressed any interest in dating since her husband left her many years ago. Some say she is afraid to get into another relationship that might hurt her. Others feel she has subconsciously waited all these years for the marriage of her ex-husband to fail. Her husband had left her for a younger woman, but all signs point to that being a stable marriage.

Her bachelor son lives with her and shows no signs of moving out. He, too, has limited interests, and offers her much comfort in their home. He works something less of a full-time job, and shows no real interest in career climbing or changing jobs. At home, he involves himself quietly with his computer and is also seemingly quite content.

If something happened where Jill needed help, she would rely on her son, her former husband, as she has for the last twelve or more years, or the married gentleman for whom she baby-sits his children. She has sufficient male support which may account for her complacency.

When she was retired out early from the company for which she was employed since her divorce, she did seemingly little to look for new employment. It was pertinment that she have an income to support herself, so many of her friends tried to steer her in the right direction.

Unemployment benefits were fairly long term to sustain her, and she was able to enjoy some months of not working at all. Then, someone set her up with a temporary job. When that assignment ended, she appeared to do little to help herself become gainfully employed; however, I may not be aware of her real efforts. She seemed to just wait until someone looked after her.

Given direction, however, Jill did well in pursuing the job she wanted, and obviously worked hard to impress the company to hire someone of her age. She was then about fifty-five years old.

When I looked for the visual image formulated of her, I found her encapsulated in a protective space suit. Her head was contained in a glass-like ball. How clearly she is shielded from the environment as she journeys safely through life!

My Friend, Mary

Sometimes my visions are not so picturesque. This one in particular is of texture. My friend, Mary, works very hard to maintain her friendships, but she can sometimes be unknowingly harsh in her manner. Her tongue may be quick to correct you on something about which she feels you have made a wrong choice, or a matter in which you did not use as excellent judgment as she.

It is sometimes important to her to express her opinion in such a manner that it comes off as "righteousness," which I am certain is not the intent. She means to be helpful in exacting terms. This also appears to satisfy an inner need to feel powerful. In actuality, she is quite perceptive and many times has very good advice.

As an aside, she describes one of her daughters in much the same way, and I presume they sometimes have difficulties with one another due to the similarities in their personalities.

I never met anyone who pushed as hard as she to accomplish all that she can in order to do a good deed or assist someone beyond her own needs. I find her efforts quite commendable, and she a faithful and entrusted friend.

When thinking of her, a texture came into my mind that was rough and rather abrasive, like sandpaper. Then the likeness of a cat's tongue came into view. By that I surmise that as a cat licks your skin in a loving way, it renders abrasiveness at the same time.

Is There A Purpose?

As you can see, I have now had countless visual imagery appear clearly in the mind's eye. I'm not at all sure why this happens or what I am supposed to do with the information. For the most part, it only gives me more definition of a person's internal self, which I may not perceive at all that well by myself.

Occasionally it is helpful for me to know what is going on with someone so that I can check on him or her to see about their well being, or perhaps counsel them in some valuable way. I have not been warned of danger in regard to anyone, so I can only surmise that I have not encountered a dangerous person. Perhaps this is a learning experience for me so that I will at some time be able to use it at a critical time.

CHAPTER THIRTEEN

The Spirit of the Crab

Matt had always been that critter in the water, resting on the board like a bump on a log. I had never defined just what kind of critter he was. I recently saw antennae on this critter and asked Gwenn what lived in the water that had antennae.

"A crab," she said, and I knew I could depend on her wealth of information that she stored impeccably.

I looked up crab in the dictionary to see if anything fit Matt's personality, and selected those things I felt most pertinent. I arranged them with a heading like this:

THE SPIRIT OF THE CRAB

Irritable and perverse in disposition
Difficult to understand, complicated
Difficult to read
To criticize, find fault

The maneuvering of an aircraft partially into a crosswind to compensate for drift
In rowing, to strike water with an oar in recovering a stroke
Or to miss it in making one

Perversity of its gait
Directed away from what is right or good

Persistent in an error or fault
Wrongly self willed or stubborn

I felt it fit. And it fit very well when this vision began to move in the water. I analyzed what I had chosen to write.

Matt was not necessarily irritable. In fact, he actually had a wonderful and kind disposition. Any irritability he may have felt was always very much contained within himself. He hid his feelings well and would give an entirely out-of-context reason for his apparent disturbance to blow you off course from the real reason of his agitation. He was complicated and difficult to read. He did, however, have wonderful communication skills when he chose to use them. He was able to delineate his point in an exacting manner.

Because my former husband never criticized me, I had been led to believe I was "perfect." I did learn from Matt that I had some faults, which were expertly described and well founded. While he rarely criticized or found fault with me, if he did, he found a way to delicately present the situation where I would be able to internalize my error and not feel adversely affected. In fact, after a fault had been pointed out, I would often catch myself repeating the error and be able to see the humor in my behavior.

In greater depth of this statement of criticism, Matt was clear to fault himself for his own expectations of perfection. He found his over-analysis to be an imperfection in himself.

The other statements in this definition related to where I felt he was emotionally and spiritually with me, as I selfishly did not feel he made the right decision to leave me. I do realize, however, that my reasons do not agree with the big plan of the almighty ruler, and He is all knowing and has made the best decision for both of us.

For some time, my thoughts often reflected back on Matt long after his leaving, and the vision of the crab continued to present itself in my mind's eye. It did not stay stagnant, and because the crab was an amphibian and could survive in water or on land, I knew it could leave this pond I envisioned it in at any time.

As I watched the vision over time, it began to be Matt, and he was walking in the water. His legs were pushing, cutting through, with a determined gait. He moved forward with a constant, steady pace, and the water was now chest high.

Days passed, and he continued to walk in my vision. Maybe weeks. One day, the water was waist high, then thigh high. Time still passed.

Gwenn told me to be ready to get a call when he was out of the water. So I watched. The water was now ankle deep, but as I continued to watch, there were apparent sand bars. The water got more shallow and then deeper at times, as he plodded along. His pace was still steady.

Days still went on, until one day he had reached a shallow plateau, and he stood in the water, shifting his weight on his feet, playing in the sand. He did not go forward. He did not come out of the water. Then he walked in the water again, thigh to ankle deep. He sat in the shallow water, and just stayed there thinking, for a couple of days.

"Contemplating his navel," I remarked to Gwenn.

She tells me he is tired.

I awakened one morning uttering these words: "Drain the pond," I said. Was I subconsciously telling Matt how to get out of the water?

In jest, I repeated the words of a "dream state" to my son that evening when he came over for dinner. I did not explain the circumstances around them. He jokingly looked out the window to the great bay upon which I live, and said, "It may take a while!"

When Matt decided to move again, he walked out of the water and strode along the beach in a straight line. He had a destination, and he was moving forward, using all the strength he had left. His pace was still determined, his gait steady.

A few days later, Gwenn asked if he was still out of the water, and I told her that he was and of his apparent destination. His life appeared to have direction, we agreed.

Shortly before Christmas I received a telephone call. It was a very warm, loving call, in that we laughed and talked for an hour, did some reminiscing, and ended with his acknowledging that I was missed.

I told Gwenn I could still see the critter resting on the board, even though Matt was out of the water. "Then he can be pulled back in," she said. And the next time I looked, he was.

It was right after the holidays that he appeared back in the water. Gwenn said that was because his family had pulled him back in, and he went back because that is where he is comfortable. He soon came out again, and the backdrop of the spirit on the board was still visible, but much more faintly.

The visions immediately following acknowledged a confused state of mind, of mentally jumping from one thing to another. I felt sorry for his state.

CHAPTER FOURTEEN

Identification with Colors, Numbers
and License Plate Lingo

I have always identified with colors, as they have had meaning to me. Many years ago, when I set up files for various subject matters at work, I most closely matched the file names with the folder or tab color that felt most comfortable. I felt they had some significance or related something to me in some way. Auras and their colors were not at all known to me at that time.

Now that I understand about auras and have learned that they have color, I am sure that someday they will have more meaning in my life. Colors will then take on new definition when I take the time to learn more about them.

One day, as a matter of personal curiosity, I began to write the letters of the alphabet and then the color that I associated with each one. I could associate most with a color. I already knew that colors portrayed our mood, as shown by what we wear. One might say we are affected by the weather; but then, doesn't the weather dictate the color of the sky, our surroundings, and the day?

Contrarily, I've always disliked working with numbers. I did very poorly in most math classes; however, I did fare well with statistics. What is worse, is that mentally distinguishing the difference between 10,000 and 100,000 was always a chore. Numbers were unimportant and difficult to remember. In terms of money and these large numbers, God has provided me with a guardian angel. Someone has certainly watched over me and guided me so that any mistakes in that regard have been minimal and not too painful.

Many years ago, the same psychic that told me my daughter was reincarnated told me that she saw "numbers, numbers, numbers" in my reading. Not just once, but twice, several years apart. Three years after the first reading, she still could not give me any interpretation of what these numbers might mean, but she did explain that she saw them. Each time we tried to identify them to something in my line of work, but I could not really associate them with anything I did or become comfortable with that attachment. I hated to work with numbers.

I don't play the lottery, either, and it has never been my desire to win or win big. Therefore there would be little likelihood that I would buy a winning ticket. I think I have too much of the "work ethic" instilled in me and enjoy the gratification of working for what I earn.

My mother told me that as a child I had repeatedly stated a set of three numbers to my father. He had played them on some check pool at work and won. The numbers were either 2, 4, 7 or 2, 4, 9. It is peculiar, now that I think about it, that those same numbers, 4, 7 and 9, have played an important part in my life in recent years. The four relates to my birthday and the nine to Matt's.

My grandmother had told me, in conversation as a young girl, that seven was her lucky number. She said it was lucky to have a seven in your phone number, address, or license plate. I remembered this advice and then adopted the seven as my own.

Of more personal interest to me are the numbers that my daughter claims have been with her through life: 24, 27, 34, 39 and 42. The 2, 4, 7 and 9 are present with an extraneous 3. Since the 3 has never been a part of my life to date, I presume that is the identifiable source of that part of her personality that is unlike any other member in the entire family. I can only assume it belongs with the soul she has carried through life along with her own.

My son's numbers, he tells me, are 8, which relates to his birth date, and 7 and 14. The 7 and 4 are again present, only he has an extraneous 1. His father's birth date is 11. I don't really know the connection, yet. At present, I am just collecting information.

The real intrigue, however, are the messages I get from reading license plates. I call this License Plate Lingo. The fact that they combine letters with numbers gives further interest. These messages, of course, are subject to my own interpretation, and I've already explained that I don't interpret well. I understand that they very well may have no validity except for amusement to myself.

I continue this rhetoric for one reason, and that is on an outside chance that I will some day learn more about what I see and feel. So far, I cannot prove or disprove anything. I can, perhaps, create enough of a story around them to peak your interest, and maybe you, the reader, will have had some similar experience or better knowledge to understand its relevance.

Long before I started trying to interpret what I saw, reading license plates amused me I don't know why. My Aunt Addie was intrigued by reading them, too, but she played the numbers that she saw in the lottery. She was a successful winner, sometimes, too, but I dare say how much she may have spent to become one.

When she was of more sound mind, I had picked her up from the nursing home one day and we discussed reading license plates and the attraction. It was not clear to her why she always read them, either. I confessed that they gave me messages. Maybe I belong with her, I don't know.

Nonetheless, since the break up of my relationship with Matt, I have sometimes gotten meaningful messages from reading these plates. It seems that for periods of time I get several messages, and then for months I get none. I did not keep a log of any kind, so will only recollect some of them. To recite all would be repetitious and boring, as this threatens to be anyway.

For the most part, earlier license plate messages told me MLE, or Matt Loves Ellen, or MLB--which I interpret to say Matt *Likes* Barb--as he had told me his relationship with her as my replacement was non-threatening to me and non-demanding of his time and/or emotions. She was merely a pleasant friend who gave him some laughs and did not expect any type of commitment. He presented her as having no attachment to him, but I know better.

I was happy with the readings for some time. Later, as the months slipped by, I read there were other women in his life. For a while, a K appeared, whom I have called Kathy. And later, a double K, with M, and the second K I've called Karen.

All of the combinations of letters are, of course, accompanied by numbers, and I have associated meanings to the numbers as well. From knowing Matt so long and doing so many things with him, I learned to know "his" numbers, and already knew mine. We did things like going to the horse races, and other things that involved numbers. The other number's meanings, well, I've just learned. I somehow have associated meanings to these numbers, but have not studied any numerology references for validity.

Some numbers I learned by card readers. One told me that both my former husband and son carried a "6," the sign of Jonah, and that was bad. Thus, "6" is the sign of the devil or otherwise some misfortune. Matt's numbers are "9 and 1," mine are "4 and 7." "0" is pretty neutral, but I have found it associated with many of Matt's numbers.

The "3's and 8's" I have learned to interpret as something to do with excessive, or ultimate, and "2's and 5's" have something to do with sharing or being equal, even as in marriage. From the combination and sequence of numbers with the letters, I get readings--left to my own interpretation, of course, which many times is less than adequate.

The discovery of the meaning of "3's and 8's" stemmed from getting a license plate message with a 3 and an 8 in it, and asking what the numbers meant. The next plate that appeared in view while driving was one containing, in some order, 380 or 830 with ULT. Obviously, they had something to do with "ultimate," I reasoned. I later expanded it to include something like "excessive," but I don't think I can distinguish whether it belongs to the 3 or 8. I just associate whatever fits at the time.

To offer some intrigue to this system, one day four months ago, a license plate message appeared before my eyes with the letters MCE. I don't recall the numbers, but they appropriately contained a "9" and a "4" with the letters to mean Matt was going to call Ellen. Now, I haven't talked to Matt on a regular basis for some time, so there was little likelihood that I would be getting a call. But I did, that very day.

I followed the subsequent messages frequently to the point of boredom, as they kept telling me the same thing about Matt and Barb, Matt and Kathy and Matt and Karen. Occasionally, they would tell me that he still loved me, and I would get some gratification in the message. I stopped consciously watching them for a while.

Then one day a new letter combination appeared. It was MLC. Carol, I called this person, but it could be Carol, Cheryl, Charlotte, or whatever you want to call her. I instinctively knew this was the new love. I also saw that Barb was out of the picture, that Kathy was okay, resembled me somewhat, and Karen was the spicy kind of gal some men need as a diversion.

Soon I learned, just after the New Year, that MWB-- Matt Was Bad! Uh huh! I knew he had crossed over the line with giving up on our relationship in his heart and had found a new lover. At one time MWB would have meant Matt with Barb, but not now. The readings of letters and numbers are most definitely subject to "feeling" as well. I took this information with some pain in my heart, and tried to discard the relevance of my "License Plate Lingo."

During one of our very few recent conversations, Matt had volunteered that he was dating a lot, and that the intimacy was not even of interest to him at that time. I took it to heart and knew that going on in that regard was next to impossible for me as well.

From the time of our separation, I have had loads of fun dating numerous nice fellows. I remember saying, "Wow, three weeks in a row I have had a date." At this time it is 35 plus weeks in a row of having fabulous, continuous, fun. Nothing serious, only two prospects of anything even remotely possible as future mates, but someone above has definitely seen to it that I have been continually entertained without the desire or necessity to be intimate.

I'm not complaining, because whatever reasons Matt has that keeps him from me have not yet been satisfied. His debts have not been paid, and I am now learning of another significant reason why he cannot return. I'm working on it with my soothsayer, Gwenn, for she is able to give me the interpretations and asks the right questions to find the deeply hidden and intricate answers.

Now, this latest reading of MWB again appeared like a neon sign. Instead of being on the back of the car where the license plate goes, it was placed in the back window of the vehicle for all to see, "MATT WAS BAD."

The events that followed are in the next chapter. Matt was bad!

I will leave you to judge the validity of the License Plate Lingo. I just don't know, but can't discard it at this point. The last readings I had were MWW, Matt was wrong, and MCE, Matt call Ellen. I'm not expecting Matt to call. Does that mean he wants to call, will call in spirit, is ignoring what he feels he should do? It's too unreliable for me, but I don't think I'll give it up yet.

CHAPTER FIFTEEN

Telepathic Transmission

I had spent the entire weekend thinking about Matt--between dates, of course, as I never had a dull weekend. That in itself is an extraordinary situation. It isn't exactly normal. I felt I had some spiritual help in this regard. All of these months I have managed to keep Matt out of my mind, but having just had a call prior to the holidays that was so loving and satisfying made him heavy on my mind. In conversation, he normally conveyed that he loved me, or otherwise implied that he did.

His conversation explicitly stated that "he couldn't have any fun anymore," because even if he went to nice places, it was time he would rather spend with me and he was always afraid he would run into me. I said I hoped I would not ever see him with someone else, and he agreed it would not do either of us any good to see the other with another companion. I reminded him that it was his choice, and we let it go and said good-bye. He had said he wanted me to know that I was missed and that he would be calling again.

My birthday immediately followed the New Year, and I expected a call from Matt to offer proper greeting. He had made such a point of my wishing him a happy birthday when I had spoken to him just prior to his birthday in September. But the call did not come. That weekend contained constant thoughts and sleepless nights, until I decided it was time that I give him a call.

I felt he must have been calling me subliminally. I would call on Sunday morning, when I thought he would be waking up.

The phone rang and rang.   Finally, a sleepy voice answered. It was his son, Joe.

"Is your dad home, I asked?" A stammering took place on the other end of the line. I could tell he was not really awake.

"I know I woke you up, but would you mind checking to see if your dad is home," I asked.

"No..o..o.   He's not home.   He's out of town, on vacation."

"Oh, I said. Well, this is Ellen, Joe. Just tell him that I called." And he said that he would. I didn't know if he would even remember the call.

Now I know Matt, and Matt does not go on vacation with anyone but a female. So I composed my thoughts in three minutes and called his car phone. I left him a sweet, seething message about how I hadn't heard from him regarding my birthday and guessed he wasn't having too much trouble with "not having any fun."

The message was delivered to his voice mailbox at 10:30 a.m.   Normally a returned call would be forthcoming within 20 minutes of my leaving a message--a telepathy, you might say. But no call, and I didn't expect one since I knew there was nothing he could say.

Knowing his habits and my intuition, he picked it up, something told me, (telepathically with a single chime that went off in my head, maybe) at 12:36 p.m., two hours later. If he had been away by himself, or another male, which he would not do, he would have called immediately.

Ten o'clock that evening, after he had taken the girl home (from a trip to Chicago, I presumed based on the time and knowing Matt), I unsuspectingly answered the telephone to hear, "Happy Birthday." I was stunned. His voice sounded as though he might have a cold, but more like he had been crying. He had been caught, and this trip was something he would not have wanted me to know about.

My reception of the call was "shocked" and unkind. I was terribly hurt, and there was nothing I could say or wanted to say about his betrayal. So I blurted out some short statements and hung up.

Still in anger, I called back and reached him on his car phone. I hastily explained I had not said what I wanted to say. He disparagingly agreed for me to go on.

"You have obviously gone on with your life just fine for yourself; now get out of mine"-- and again I hung up as to not get into discussion over what had happened.

I knew what had happened. He had telepathically been contacting me. Our souls were connected, as Gwenn has told me several times, and he was unable to get away from me. I called Gwenn immediately, and we reasoned he deserved the statement. I could no longer tolerate the phone calls that were hypocritical to what was going on in his life.

I was crushed. The bond that we had, the love I knew was there had been betrayed. He had crossed over the line. And the last phone call from him not more than a week and a half ago, of "he can't have any fun any more" and how I was missed took on new light.

It was not like Matt to lie, as he spoke from his heart. I knew he had tried to overcome his conscience of feelings toward me and was trying to be happy going on with his life. But he must have been calling out to me all weekend, in some way, and I had heard him. And that's why I called.

I was in emotional pain for the next several days or more. I understood what had happened, that his feelings were still there for me, but so was the betrayal--a great scar had been made.

I was home from work sick the following two days, but unrelated to this incident. It did give me more than ample time to think, however, and to rest, which needed for both reasons.

Upon waking up from a nap one afternoon, I felt such a warm feeling in my chest. It was the same feeling I carried always when Matt was in my life, and a remembrance of the love I felt for him in that relationship. It felt so good, I did not want to let it go. It was so familiar; my whole body filled with love for him. As my thoughts drifted, I felt him make love to me, and caress me. I knew it was what he felt, and was probably feeling then.

It was so real, I believe it really happened telepathically. He was really in my life for that treasured point in time, even though we could not share a real relationship now. It was a telepathic transmission of love, and I accepted it warmly.

CHAPTER SIXTEEN

A Love Story of Two Souls

Still plagued by my attachment to Matt, and his apparent going on with his life without me, Gwenn and I talked about the dynamics of what was really at play at the time he wished to take an "intermission" from me. She, too, feels the connectivity between Matt and myself, and in fact has been a strong influence in convincing me that what I feel exists does in fact exist for both Matt and myself.

Being the realist she is, it is astonishing to me that Gwenn has such a reach for the supernatural powers. She has studied them through her training in psychology and with the police force in various capacities. She supports her feelings with stated facts of experiments in which energy transmissions had actually taken place. Only because Gwenn is so "black and white" and factual do I believe her.

In discussion, she will often ask me a question. When I am able to come up with the answer, the result is a profound truth. She said that Matt and I had a partnership up to some point in the relationship, and then it broke down. This is the second major reason for the demise of my relationship with Matt. There was a turning point where the partnership no longer existed. She asked me to think back to the point where that happened.

At first I drew a blank, but within moments knew the exact point. It was when he had finally made a break from his marriage. He had moved his wife out of the house, which was her choice, and was within a few days after Christmas. This was an extremely big step and at a difficult time. I was pleased at the event as it had needed to happen for a long, long while.

However, soon after, I made a demand that he had better file for divorce within some specifically stated time, like 3 months, or 6 months, I don't recall. That was the breaking point. He told me at the time, more than once, that it had done something to the relationship. He wasn't sure what, but I think he even stated he felt emasculated by it. I really did not understand it, but I did remember.

Gwenn's response to that was this. "Matt wants to come back to you, but on equal terms. He feels you have *power* over him, and that is not comfortable to him. He does not want to overpower you; he wants to be equal with you."

I knew we had now hit on a second very big point in the break up of the relationship: 1) the first being his having family debts to pay (and obviously needing to pay them alone to prove his strength), and now; 2) his need to regain his energy level and strength to equal the power he feels I have over him.

In fact, in one of our recent conversations, he expressed how he still, after these months of separation, got shaky and out of control in seeing me. The loss of composure had given him a loss of masculinity, and where I found it adorable knowing the depth of the feelings in his soul, he found it emasculating. It does not seem to matter that I believe my feelings are just as deep for him.

Now I have the predicament that I have told him to stay out of my life, and I don't feel it is the right thing to do to call to say that I now understand this second point.

Before I could complete the thought, Gwenn interjected, "You will have to tell him that you understand, and that he has to forgive you for your power in the demand you made of him before the two of you can go on-- telepathically. He has to regain that strength that he has lost before he can have a relationship with you and feel your equal."

I thought about what she said for a few days, wondering how and when my mental messages would ever be received. It was also unclear to me how he would ever get that power. I found myself making internal demands constantly, in terms of threats. It was my way of setting deadlines for myself, and mentally for others. "You had better do this by that date, or that had better take place by a specific time." I think it comes from working in Project Management--have a realistic goal, set a time frame, and meet it.

I said to Gwenn, "Do I need to change to make that work, because I don't think I can."

"No, she said. Matt loves you for your strength. He would not want you to change. It's just that he has lost his, and cannot have a relationship with you without feeling equal."

One evening, after going to bed, my thoughts were on how Matt would get this power back. I reflected on a story I had heard one time about someone at work not having the "authority" to make a decision. That person was meeting with his boss who had asked him if he had done a certain thing in regard to an assignment. The subordinate replied that he did not have the authority. So the boss took out a scrap of paper and wrote "authority" on it and handed it to his employee. He then proceeded to tell him to put it in his pocket, so that he always had "authority." I thought, I wish it could be that simple.

I no sooner thought that, when I went into a concentrated state of mind, and energy began to flow from my swelled chest, sending "power and strength." The sending went on and on, without any conscious, premeditated thought on my part. It continued until such a time I became frightened that I would send all that I had, and would leave myself none. So I stopped it, as to not deplete my entire supply.

A couple of days later, I took a mental vision of Matt. I found him standing with a round metal plate over his chest, with hands beating softly and ever so slowly on the plate. He had received the message, but was still exhausted. At one point I saw him sit down and lay back. Gwenn said, "He has received the power and strength, but doesn't know where it came from and is too tired to use it."

CHAPTER SEVENTEEN

Trouble Brewing

After many years of diligent service for a major corporation, I was disillusioned to think that I had earned the respect of my peers and other members of management. After attaining the first level of management, I thought "I was in." I thought I was part of a management team that would support me and lead me through the ranks of success. Was I mistaken!

It was cut throat from the very beginning. Several similarly titled managers resented my having obtained the position and status of manager. Some males, particularly, felt threatened. I can't begin to tell you of the petty things that went on, like measuring my office size to see that it was no larger than theirs, and eliminating my name from important meeting notices, and so on.

I fought this battleground for two to three years, when trouble really started to brew. Background noise began to erupt that I had made this mistake or that, and it found its way to my boss by special meeting of one of my more vicious counterparts.

As an example of the poor management on the part of the corporation was that I later learned a subsequent large-scale meeting had been held with my peers about me without my knowledge. I can just imagine the things that were said since I was not there to defend myself.

Soon the management of the car group that I was working for began treating me differently, as if I were inept, as they had information about me, even if erroneous, that I was not privy to. I was obviously being put to the test, felt the stress, and my inadequacies, as if by design, began to erupt. In one meeting I attended, one of the manager's slipped and referred to my incompetency.

As a result, and not immediately, a footlocker of information was being collected against me. After having been promised a new job as a result of some reorganization, it was retracted, I was demoted, and given a lowly job.

This was my set of circumstances, but the particulars for several other persons in this division must have had similar governing factors. I was demoted on November 1 because the new job I had been offered was to start November 1. Six others were demoted on December 1 I was to later find out.

This was obviously a corporate movement, not really based on a persons personal merits. It just needed some fuel to start the burning process. I learned not to take it personally after I fought long and hard to gain back my self respect and file a judgment against the corporation and the manager responsible for my position.

Because all of us victims were over forty years of age, our health, in many regards, was at risk. More than half of the others in this same situation had resultant heart attacks, for which they can thank their employer. I had no severe heart problems, thankfully; however, the long duration of the event to consummation left me with a nervous twitch which I will probably have with me for life. It actually is an involuntary spasm that occurs in my extremities.

What I won was not my position and level back, as the corporation would never admit to having been wrong. However, I did win a settlement, a forced retirement with normal pension, and most importantly, my self respect. It was worth the fight, as I can hold my head up high and be proud that I was successful in taking on a large corporation with the help of my expert counsel, Gwenn, and a wonderful attorney.

CHAPTER EIGHTEEN

The Demon in the Shower

One morning, while taking my shower, thoughts of Sue entered my mind. That tree trunk-like thing I envisioned around her must be an evil spirit of sorts, I reasoned, and I saw deep roots, like crows feet. I wonder if I have an evil spirit, I thought, and she appeared.

About two feet in length, elongated, like the size of a two-by-four, was this creature. She appeared to be female, and dressed like the Blessed Mother, only in black and gray, maybe with some white. Her nose, however, was long and hooked, like that of a witch. "A combination of good and evil," I surmised. Gwenn had some other suitable interpretation, but it did not mirror mine at all.

I addressed this demon by asking if she had anything to do with Rob, Sue's late husband, who had committed suicide. Nothing happened. The thought crossed my mind about my unfortunate situation with Hometown Motors, my employer of many years, and with whom I had enjoined in a lawsuit. Why I said "Hometown Motors," in my mind, I don't know, as it was such a remote thought; it did not even exist in my conscious mind. But when I did, the demon sprinted away.

I told Gwenn that I had seen my demon. "Oh, really, she said."

"Yes," I replied. "But when I said 'Hometown Motors,' it ran."

"Do you know why?" she asked.

"No," I said.

She explained, "They don't like to be called by their real name, and you have named it."

The demon appeared many times since, but never to alarm me. It was just an annoyance, a nuisance. Sometimes it felt like there were four hands washing my back instead of two, or I just felt its presence while in the shower. Water may somehow be my "conduit" or means of communication, I reasoned. I recall feeling like I had extra hands while I was resting in bed, but only once.

Gwenn asked many times about my encounters with this demon and if it was still present. It usually was. Once it appeared in the form of a raven, or was perhaps a second demon, which I have rationalized might be connected to the deep roots, or crows feet of Sue's tree trunk.

As my case progressed with Hometown Motors, the demon was still present. A mediation of the case took place, and either side had the opportunity to "accept" or "reject." Up until the decisions were made regarding mediation, the demon persisted. Since then, the demon has gone away or has taken a sabbatical.

In regard to my demon having the dress likeness to the Blessed Mother, well, she has a story of her own. I am not at all clear on its connectivity at this point in time. There was a resemblance to her familiar caped dress except for the color; I had told Gwenn that I had always seen the Blessed Mother in blue and white. It was not clear to me why there would be a color change.

I said, "I don't remember ever seeing anything else dressed in a similar caped attire."

"The Grim Ripper," she said, and we laughed.

When my Aunt Addie was diagnosed with Alziemers and put into a nursing home, her son passed on a few of her belongings to me. One item was a small statue of the Blessed Mother. I had never had anything like that, and because it was hers, even though it was old and chipped, I cherished having it. Because of its tattered condition, I placed it in a cabinet in my living room for a long time.

One day I decided I should put it away, and I carefully wrapped it in tissue paper and placed it in a very good box which I put in the nightstand next to my bed. One night I touched the headboard, and I heard a strange squeak. I touched it again, and it squeaked again.

While the sound came from that direction it did not seem to be the headboard squeaking. I got out of bed, went to the side where the squeaking was taking place, and again wriggled the headboard to find out where the noise was coming from. It did not squeak. I tried again, but could not get it to make any noise. I got back into bed and tried moving the headboard again, but nothing happened. I tried again the following morning, and still nothing.

The thought crossed my mind that I had put the Blessed Mother statue away in a box, and I bet that I had put it in the nightstand where the squeaking appeared to be taking place. When I remembered again, I looked in the nightstand, and it was there.

I told Gwenn about this squeaking noise, and she then explained. "It's the Blessed Mother," she said. "Take her out of the box."

"Take her out of the box?" I asked.

"Yes, take her out of the box. She wants to help you, and she can't do it from there. Put her somewhere where she can see you."

So I did. She is now sitting in plain view on my chest of drawers. As I walked away, I heard a small "peep." I think she thanked me.

Since then, I have occasionally heard a small "peep" or "squeak" upon walking into the bathroom. I find it hard to believe that my tile on a cement floor is squeaking, but somehow it occasionally does. And I say to the Blessed Mother, I know you are with me and I thank you.

"Do you have a cross that you can put on?" Gwenn asked.

"I have one that Aunt Addie gave me, I said. But it doesn't have a chain. Maybe I have a chain I bought for her once. I'll try to find it."

"Wear the cross," she said.

So I found the cross and the chain and put it on. I still saw the demon, and it was still not frightening. It changed nothing, but maybe I felt more protected.

All has been quiet since the mediation.

CHAPTER NINETEEN

Just Plain Buggy

It was someone's witchcraft or I had gone just plain "buggy." The logical explanation was this. It was spring, and I was having my house painted. It's exterior was cedar, which was covering cinderblock, the home's original structure.

When the painter arrived, he told me he would first scrape off the old, loose paint, and then caulk. Then I could select the color I wanted, and my home would look fresh and new. Since the work was being done on the outside, it was not necessary that I even be home.

One evening after work, I needed something out of one of the back rooms of the house. It was probably something from my sewing and craft room, as I was usually working on some project. When I left the room, I found my feet were crawling with bugs.

I quickly brushed them off my feet and ankles, and dared go back there again with some hefty bug spray in my hand. Again my legs became covered with bugs. I sprayed my self as well as the carpeting, but the poison did not seem to deter them from hanging onto my legs.

I got out of the room as quickly as possible. It was as though I was watching a horror movie, only it was really happening.

This time I went back into the room better prepared. I had to kill those things off, or die! I put on white knee socks so I could see when they got onto my legs. In that way maybe I would find where they were in the room. Again, my feet and legs became covered, and again I sprayed a deadly spray over the entire carpeting.

Since this was my sewing and craft room, the entire closet was completely packed with materials and crafting supplies. I could only imagine what the inside of the closet had in store for me since it could only offer wonderful nesting space and great hibernation for bugs.

I went back into the adjoining hallway to adjust the thermostat to find that the bugs were there as well. I was still fighting them off and spraying for all I was worth. My next step was to set off those aerosol cans of bug bombs in the house before I left for work in the morning. I did this, which gave me some peace of mind, knowing that I would still have to go through closets later to make sure that I had gotten them all.

With this job done, I proceeded to do the next chore. Sure enough, the bugs had infiltrated into my fabrics, and were visually easy to see in the packages of white batting used for crafting. I began throwing out what was infested, and salvaged what I could. In handling the cotton stuffing material, I felt my hands were being eaten alive. I felt a sharp, tearing sting when I could see nothing. This was a real nightmare.

Since there was a sewing club meeting at one of the girl's homes that week, I packed up the materials I needed that were still good for a project I wanted to do. I was spread out on the floor of my friend's home when I could feel this same bug sting attack me. I was horrified to think that I had possibly brought these culprits into her home. She had a new grandchild visiting quite frequently, and my thoughts immediately went to that new baby. I grimaced at the thought. Nothing was ever said, so I can only hope that nothing happened.

My nightmare did not end, however. The bugs continued to come into my home, and I felt I had been cursed. It wasn't until a conversation I had with Gwenn that I gleaned information that clarified what was happening.

She at one time had carpenter ants in her house from a big tree near her yard, and had hired an exterminator service to treat her home. The process entailed drilling holes into the exterior of her home to insert the poisonous solution.

When she later had the holes caulked, she, too, had bugs come into her home. She described them as being ankle deep in her home, too. They, like the bugs at my house, had become trapped in the walls and could not get out. So they came in!

They now had migrated into all of my rooms. They were in my clothes, in my drawers, in my bed and in the toilet. I had now bombed the house twice and had gone through three gallons of commercial grade bug spray from a local exterminator. I was driving myself and everyone around me mad.

I had my son come over and help me turn my mattress over so I could spray both sides. He also helped by cleaning crevices I could not reach on my own as I cleaned toilets and various other places bugs would hide. I threw out talcum powders, flour, and anything else I thought might house such varmints.

One evening I found them in the bathtub with me, appearing to have come from a very private area. That caused me to go to a gynecologist on an emergency appointment on lunch hour the next day, as I was sure I was infested as well.

"So you think you have crabs," the nurse said.

"No, I don't," I said with alarm. "I think I have household bugs!"

"Sure," she and the doctor both thought!

It turned out I had none.

My body would feel fine when I put my clothes on, but at some point during the day or evening, I would feel as though bugs were in them and had come alive. I could feel bugs in them, but could not see them. I was washing everything I owned in bleach, and still I felt I could not rid myself of them.

My skin crawled with bugs. My family doctor treated me with two prescriptions of something that would kill out any such intruder, but when I still complained, he suggested I see a dermatologist. I did.

The derm said, "Bugs cannot pierce the skin," as I was claiming them to do. She kindly explained that my nerve endings were so distressed that they made me feel as though I had bugs. And the "stringy" white stuff I had oozing from my face was a result of my constant picking and was normal. It was supposed to be there. I had just upset the natural balance of my skin.

Seeing me in a paranoid state, she gave me some soaps and creams for sensitive skin. She also thought I was nuts, charged me seventy-five dollars for a five-minute visit, and sent me on my way.

I was nuts. I had gone mad. I was cleaning out drawers with bleach, soaking and washing every belt, every pair of gloves and every pair of shoes. It was a monumental task. I did this for three months straight. I could see little dark spots and white spots everywhere. They were in my car, too. I was even asking the exterminator to look in my car to see if he could find termites.

I was spraying my car. I was spraying my clothes. I was spraying me. I carried a small bottle of spray with me everywhere. I was inhaling the stuff.

I watched dust float, and looked for bugs in the dust. I could see red particles in the dust in the sunlight. I was sure it had life. I was obsessed. I was also possessed. I felt that I had been cursed.

One day when I was washing my hands in the bathroom, a piece of porcelain enamel flaked off the side of the bowl and landed in the sink. I was sure some demon was responsible for this as well, as it was not a normal occurrence. I was continually looking for life forms in the crevices of the counter and in the air, and I was sure bugs had eaten the enamel off the sink to cause the flaking.

At first I thought the flaked piece had come from the overflow drain in the bowl's side, but in checking, it had not. It was close to there, but it was from a completely finished area and had found reason to come loose and fall off.

Why was this demon so intent on persecuting me? Why wouldn't it go away? Was it because I was not afraid of her? While the reasons for all of these happenings might be logically explained, I considered this was her way of getting to me. It just didn't seem possible that it could be normal.

CHAPTER TWENTY

Telepathic Messages

We have identified on a wavelength in its elementary stages. Only this morning, I had been up about a half hour when a strong, commanding thought crossed my mind. It was one of those demands like, "You had better do that within this time frame." This habit is one I wanted to particularly avoid with Matt at this point in time--and I immediately laughed, and said to myself, "Strike that thought, I didn't mean it!"

I then wanted to tell this to Gwenn, but knew she was at work. I was not, so I sent her a telepathic message, wondering if she would get it. I reasoned, if she was really busy, she would not.

My telephone rang within one to two minutes. It was Gwenn. I queried, "Did you get my call?"

"No," she said.

"I mean telepathically."

"When did you send it?" she asked.

"Minutes ago, maybe two," I replied.

"I must have," she said. "I am knee deep in alligators, and the thought crossed my mind that you were home at this time and I should call you."

CHAPTER TWENTY-ONE

Letting Go of a Loved One

Last evening I had a date with a new gentleman, Steve, who met all the requirements of a potentially worthy relationship. We had gone to the same high school, were raised on the same side of town, and each worked independently to bring ourselves up to a commendable status in life. He was extremely attractive to me.

The evening went well, and brought forth an invitation for not one date for next weekend, but two. I am enamored and feel the strong possibility that something may develop between us, if not for permanency, for an interval that might serve each of our purposes well. For you see, he is in the process of divorce, and certainly a long time from real emotional stability or knowing what he wants. And I, still in love with Matt, do not know how far I should let this go if it in fact develops. I surely do not want a repeat of a fourteen-year courtship with my mate walking away when the final papers are signed.

So, this morning was a melancholy kind of day, with me not wanting to bound out of bed as normal, and not wanting to begin my day. I had a need to totally relax on the couch with a quiet, sorting, thinking process taking place. I was so saddened to feel the start of a letting go process begin. Was it healthier than hanging on to a love I knew existed between two people that could not be consummated? Probably. Was I ready to enter into another relationship that may lead to being hurt? Did I see it as a nice interim companionship while all three of us worked to get our lives on an even plain again? I did not know, but it was painful. It was a sad day.

I turned off the stereo and concentrated on a heart to heart mental conversation with Matt. I explained how deeply I loved him and my current, heartsick feeling of letting go. I told him I understood he had not forgiven me for my power over him in the relationship, and that I had not meant for that to happen. I said his loss of power was a result of the powerlessness he felt in the loss of his marriage, and that some day he would get that strength back. I expressed how I felt with the painfulness of letting go and having the insight and visualization of a potential mate with whom to share myself and my feelings. I asked if he needed me to let him go. I also explained that I selfishly did not wish him well in a new love, or to find happiness without me, and that I hoped "Brady," my favorite horoscope writer, was right in that his life in 1996 would "suck." I found a deep need to ask him what I should do. And I asked him please to let me know.

This is the same day. I did not know how I would get my answer. It was too soon to begin to even question when. Sometime this afternoon the feeling crossed my mind that Matt and I were still married in heart and soul, even if we were not ever really married. It was later that evening, while having dinner by myself, that some small thought of Matt passed through my mind--and then I dismissed all thoughts of him.

As I ate, with silverware in my right hand, the fingers of my left hand were clenched, and I knew instinctively, without looking, that my fingers were closed in the same way Matt's were clenched many times while he ate. It felt how Matt's hand felt, not mine. I could then feel Matt's hand instead of mine. How would I even know how Matt's hand felt in that position? I knew. Was his hand mine? I felt his hand, not mine. Were we as one?

I had my sign. It told me Matt and I would be together again; that I did not need to let go. I felt such relief, until I realized he did not give me full direction. Or did he? I had to think. I wanted to believe Matt and I would be together, in hand, as we are in heart and soul. He did not tell me what I should do with my life in the interim, or if he would be with me in spirit only.

I got the feeling that Matt would be back, but not soon, and I should let my life go on naturally, pursue a relationship if it happened for me, and Matt would always be with me. Maybe that means spiritually only, but it gave me confirmation that we are one.

I later called Gwenn to tell her about my day. Her interpretation was always very important to me, and this time quite similar. It said to her, "I will never let go of you; I will be back." She felt that he still had work to do (emotional, spiritual, life-debt work), but he would be back. I should go on with my life and not worry about it.

"You're beginning to interpret," she told me.

After that experience, I took Matt's rosary out of the drawer and placed it by my bed. I would sleep with it until such time that I felt it was no longer appropriate for me to do so.

CHAPTER TWENTY-TWO

I've Got You Under My Skin

One day while talking on the telephone with Gwenn, she asked me to take a reading of Rob, Sue's late husband. Before I could, I got a reading of Matt. Gwenn was still talking, and I broke in, "Gwenn, what is Matt doing trying to get out of his skin? He is wiggling and pulling."

"He is trying to get rid of you. You are under his skin."

She recited the song to me, made famous by Keely Smith in the fifties, and with each word, she knew she was right.

> I've got you under my skin
> I've got you deep in the heart of me
> So deep in my heart
> You're really a part of me
> I've got you under my skin
>
> The very thought of you
> Makes me stop
> Before I begin
> I've got you under my skin

He struggled with that skin for the entire day. By the next morning, I could see that he was exhausted, and was just sitting. I couldn't tell if he was completely finished, but I didn't think so.

I again reported in to Gwenn, who said, "No, he isn't finished, and he doesn't know if he wants to. He doesn't want to lose you."

Each day seemed to bring an entirely new vision, but after all, it had been a traumatic event with me finding out about his weekend vacation with some lady.

Next I saw Matt eating a hamburger. He was just chewing on that hamburger all day. I said to Gwenn, "This one I think I can figure out myself. He's really chewing on things, thinking them over."

"Yes," she said. "And the meat is the real meat of the issue."

The visions are coming more frequently now, and changing by the day, as one changes their feelings on a subject matter after pondering or thinking it over. Some things require more thought and take more time to settle in comfortably. And since the visions are purely symbolic, you can see how strange they can become.

Matt was not alone in his feelings of being obsessed by me. Since Matt was constantly on my mind now, I was obsessed by him. I'm sure I drove Gwenn nearly mad with my visions and questions.

The most recent vision of Matt was this. Symbols banging, whistles blowing, the marching band playing

da da da   da da da   da da da
da da da   da da da   da da da da

I most definitely had to ask Gwenn for definition as to the other sounds in my head as the band played on.

She said, "That is a marching song from John Philip Sousa; however, if you can remember, it was the Morgan High School song. Think about it, and the end verse."

Gwenn, Steve and I had gone to the same school and Matt had now definitely gotten the message about Steve. The words of the Morgan High School song go like this:

Be kind to your web footed friends
For a duck may be somebody's mother
They live all year round in the swamp
Where the weather is cold and damp

Now you may think this is the end
But it's not

CHAPTER TWENTY-THREE

A Call to Answer

I had been warned by Gwenn to block thoughts of Matt because the sending of messages back and forth would drive each other crazy. I was sure they were driving her crazy, too, because she had to listen to me. I had fully intended to work on that.

On my way home from work today, my thoughts wee melancholy on Steve and the potential relationship. I felt very drawn to him, or at least to see what was there for me. A disappointing thought was that he would not retain the same interest, and I would be left empty again, even if still dating others steadily. My thoughts of Matt were certainly not far from reach; it was just that he was unobtainable. I looked forward to seeing Steve this weekend, and that good looking face of his.

I read my license plate messages, which were telling me the normal things that were going on with Karen and Carol, and especially how each were questioning Matt. I suppose he may be acting peculiarly. Another surprising message was for me to be very protective, but of what I'm not sure. I lost track of the thought and did not pursue further messages. In time I should ignore these readings, too, as they are all telling me about Matt.

A heavy feeling came over me in regard to Steve, but I could not figure out why. So far he had not had the opportunity to hurt me, but that is what I felt the heaviness was all about. It was very puzzling.

When I got home, and was in the middle of fixing dinner, the callings seemed so strong and frequent. I was compelled to answer what I felt was a deep need of Matt to converse with me. He was in desperate pain since he had told me to go on, and was suffering over the interest I had in Steve. That may have been the heavy feeling I had in my stomach in regard to Steve. He wanted to know if he should come back to me, and was asking me what to do.

I had to answer. He had never left a call from me unanswered, either by telephone or now telepathically, and I could not bare to feel his pain any longer. I stopped what I was doing and went directly to my couch and began to close out other thoughts. The house was quiet, and I was alone, so there was no problem taking the opportunity to communicate.

As soon as I began to concentrate on my thoughts, by chest began to fill. The feeling got stronger and my chest grew bigger and bigger, frightening me. I thought it would explode. I was about to transmit telepathically, and I knew it. My message went like this:

Matt, I love you so dearly. And I smothered him with kisses, all over his body. I enveloped him in my emotion for him. I particularly concentrated around his neck, without any preconceived objective, thinking that if he were to receive "a sign," it would somehow be related to that spot on his neck. I may even have left a "red spot" from the strength of the kiss I drew from him. He was feeling pain about allowing me to go to someone else, and he wanted to know if he should come back to me now.

I told him if it was not right to come back now, that he should not. I wanted to say that he should come back now, and we would work things out together, but feelings for Steve got in the way, and I held back. I was not sure I wanted to trade a potential relationship with Steve for a trying, painful relationship with Matt when he wasn't ready. I told him he had to forgive me for unintentionally overpowering and emasculating him before we could go on, and I assured him that I loved him and that it would be all right.

Transmission over.

I knew the strength and power I had went beyond the first demand that emasculated him; it was the way in which I took over all of his weaknesses and his family's problems. I verbally solved them for him and made him feel incapable. In his current state, he did not have the know how or strength to forge ahead with these things himself.

I asked Gwenn if he ever was that strong, and she told me yes. Then I recalled how much I leaned on his strength to help me through countless problems during and after my divorce. Now his divorce had left him bereft, and my overbearing power had taken that strength from him. No wonder he could not put a life together with me until he was certain that his strength equaled mine.

I felt a peace between us for the rest of the evening and through the night. The next day, however, around noon, I felt the peace may even let each of us go on independently with our lives, and a mild depression set in. I just wasn't sure if it was my depression or his. I feel it is difficult to discern at this point.

I asked Gwenn if the swelling I felt take place in my chest was a normal occurrence of such a transmission, as I had experienced it twice, now. She said that it was a perception, and not a reality. It was just a focal point for me, and that is where I felt it.

She also mentioned that Matt may not have realized he actually received a telepathic message. He may have surmised it was his own thinking. I said that I felt as though the communication was "on line"-- as it was happening. She said that it may have been, providing both of us were in a mental state to send and receive. The best time was at a time of relaxation, just before going to sleep, or while in a meditative state.

I then asked why, when I had sent a message to Matt at 10:30 a.m. it took him until 5:30 that evening to respond.

She laughed. "It was sitting in cue on his answering machine. He wasn't able to receive it until later, or he was pondering it--but most likely was preoccupied and did not get it right away. It would not have been received until such a time that he was mentally able to accept the message."

CHAPTER TWENTY-FOUR

Closure

To date, several months later, Matt and I have had no communication personally or telepathically. I suspect he is not out of my life forever. My expectation is that he will not appear again for another year or more. It is inexplicable how fate has it that someone in your own neighborhood range, say within ten minutes from your home, can not appear in your life for years. One might think that you would at least see that person on the street or at a local store or restaurant from time to time. Others, while not even geographically convenient to you might appear at some remote place and on more than one occasion.

Brenda, my former neighbor and trusted card reader, had told me something many months ago in a Tarot card reading. Even she mistrusted what she had seen in the last card read. She stopped, put the card down and then looked at it again in disbelief. She had always seen Matt swinging like a pendulum in trying to make a decision. She had always received signs that Matt was one who was filled with empty promises.

She hesitated thoughtfully before telling me what she saw. She spoke carefully, showing doubt and skepticism by her demeanor. She then told me that Matt would finally come back into my life and ask for me, but I would then be in a position to have to make a choice.

ABOUT THE AUTHOR

Ellen Blend was born in Michigan and was raised there her entire life, except for a short segment of time in which she lived in California. She was only six months old, then. Her father had tried to get work there during hard times, but when unsuccessful, returned the family to Michigan.

She led a quiet childhood, without any brothers or sisters; however, she was raised for most of her younger years across the street from a female cousin, just two years older than she.

Ellen's father was her mother's second husband. The first marriage was to a man who was not ready to settle down, and who decided not to come home most of their married life. They divorced, and at the age of 27, she married Ellen's father, aged 40. Having one child seemed suitable for that time in their lives.

Her mother's sister, with whom her mother was quite close, also married and had one child, the cousin with whom Ellen was raised.

Her family life consisted of a small nucleus of eight people: her mother, father, aunt, uncle, cousin and grandparents, who were the sister's parents. The parents on the fathers' sides seemed insignificant in both family units.

Much later in life Ellen learned that her grandfather was not her mother's real father. The girls were always treated equally, and neither were the wiser during childhood. It wasn't until there was some discrepancy found on her mother's birth certificate, an age correction not clearly explained, that raised a question. She appeared to be favored by her father, so no one would ever have suspicioned this to be so.

As a young child, even though Ellen was raised in a normal family setting with good parents, she feared her mother. There was a tension in the house that was very uncomfortable due to her mother's extreme nervousness.

Ellen's father had a severe illness with ulcers. Her mother worked to help out the family, but the stress and tension was too much for her and her demeanor deteriorated; her aura blackened.

She would fix Ellen a good breakfast before sending her off to school, but the uneasiness in the house was severe. Many mornings, Ellen felt unloved. She actually feared her mother might poison her.

It wasn't until her early teenage years, during which time her father died of a heart attack, that she and her mother resumed a good relationship. During those difficult years, when most parent-child relationships become more strained, they were the closest and shared a lot of love.

When Ellen began dating, the relationship began to change again. Her mother became jealous of her male companions and the loss of personal attention. She began to create a wall between them. When she became unhappy with one of Ellen's male friends, she threw her out of the house, forcing her to move in with a girlfriend.

When Ellen decided to marry, the relationship with her mother was still damaged, and that closeness never returned. Her mother stayed jealous of Ellen's possessions, never became a close grandmother to her children, and caused so much discomfort at holiday functions that Ellen finally excluded her.

Her mother did remarry, which brought happiness back into her life for a period of fourteen years. She and Ellen never fully mended their relationship. It ended at her mother's death with an acceptance of their relationship in disrepair and without remorse.

As an adult, and while married, Ellen continued her education. She returned to college when her children were about 9 and 10 years of age. As they grew older, she increased her night school attendance and completed a bachelor's degree at what was then called Lawrence Institute of Technology. Later, with a failing marriage, she went on to complete her master's degree at an extension center of Central Michigan University.

Today she lives alone in a moderately kept home on Anchor Bay of Lake St. Clair which she claims gives her much solace and pleasure. It is there that she found the time to document the visions and spiritual encounters that have been with her through much of her adult life. She hopes that you have enjoyed reading about them.

www.ingramcontent.com/pod-product-compliance
Lightning Source LLC
Chambersburg PA
CBHW072011040426
42447CB00009B/1587